MAKING SENSE OF IT ALL

Making Sense of It All

Pascal and the Meaning of Life

Thomas V. Morris

WILLIAM B. EERDMANS PUBLISHING COMPANY
GRAND RAPIDS, MICHIGAN

© 1992 by Wm. B. Eerdmans Publishing Co.

2140 Oak Industrial Drive N.E., Grand Rapids, Mich. 49505 /

P.O. Box 163, Cambridge CB3 9PU U.K.

Printed in the United States of America

12 11 10 09 08 07   14 13 12 11 10 9

Library of Congress Cataloging-in-Publication Data

Morris, Thomas V.

Making sense of it all : Pascal and the meaning of life /

Thomas V. Morris.

p.   cm.

Includes index.

ISBN 978-0-8028-0652-9 (pbk.)

1. Philosophy — Introductions. 2. God. 3. Conduct of life.

4. Pascal, Blaise, 1623-1662. I. Title.

BD21.M645   1992

100—dc20   92-29600

                                          CIP

www.eerdmans.com

To the Pascalians:
May you flourish day to day!

TENTS

CONTENTS

PREFACE

I AM very excited about the ideas in this book. They were developed over the last seven years as I read and discussed the extraordinarily stimulating and insightful writings of Blaise Pascal with some of the best schoolteachers in this country. From elementary schools, middle schools, junior highs, high schools, prep schools, public, private, and parochial settings, these intelligent, mature, searching, and enthusiastic people have come to Notre Dame for a month during the summer to philosophize and cavort, to renew their energies, reestablish their priorities, and expand their vision of the greatest human efforts ever made to understand what this life is all about.

Summer after summer, groups of fifteen have descended on South Bend under the sponsorship of the National Endowment for the Humanities program of Summer Seminars for School Teachers, a program that builds bridges between our colleges and universities and our school systems. The many teachers I have met and gotten to know in this program have been an inspiration to me. I thank them for all their questions and ideas, which have helped me, a philosopher, to come to see more deeply the true importance of philosophical thinking for every intelligent person. They have given me insight, they have given me energy, and one group even gave me the beautiful Montblanc Diplomat fountain pen with which I have written this book. To all of my Pascalians it is dedicated with great affection and gratitude.

I

OUR NEED FOR A GUIDE

WHEN you stop to think about it, life can be very confus-
ing. Imagine yourself a victim of amnesia suddenly
awakening from a deep sleep in the midst of some vast forest.
Looking around, it seems that you are equipped for a journey
of some kind, but you realize to your utter astonishment that
you have no idea where you came from, how you got here,
where in the world you are, or where you're going. You have
no map or compass. And your surroundings seem, in various
ways, very strange, even dangerous. If someone else were to
appear on the scene who seemed to understand your situation
and to have answers for all your questions, you'd listen. At least,
if I were in such a position, *I* certainly would. And if this person
described the location of our immediate environs in a way that
made sense of what I could see and hear around me, I'd listen
all the more intently to what he had to say about my origins,
mission, and destination. I hope you would too.

This, of course, is a simple image of the human condition.
For the most part, we sleepwalk through life. When something
does happen to awaken us from our slumber, we sit befuddled,
disoriented, perplexed. If someone comes along who seems to
be able to help make sense of our situation, it is only reasonable

1

that we should listen. One such person is the great seventeenth-century scientist and mathematician Blaise Pascal. In his *Pensées* (pronounced "Pon-sayz"; a rough English translation would be *Thoughts*) we have the notes for a book he intended to write, a book that was meant to provide us with that map and compass we so desperately need. The book was never written. Death intervened. But the notes themselves evince such a profound cartography of the spirit that, after three hundred years, the *Pensées* remains a perennial bestseller. These scintillating and often profound reflections on such topics as the human quest for a happy life, the greatness and wretchedness of the human condition, the nature of faith, the hiddenness of God, and the cogency of a religious worldview constitute a philosophical bequest capable of changing people's lives. I've seen it happen. Mature, intelligent people who have lived long enough to re-alize how little they know about what really matters in life find in Pascal's thoughts exciting new perspectives and directions for their own thinking. Many people who have almost given up trying to make much sense of their lives find in these notes enough clues, hints, and flashes of insight to spur them on and renew their quest to make sense of it all.

In this book I want to explore with Pascal those most important questions for getting our bearings. This will not be a book about Pascal. There are many fascinating studies of his life. Nor will it be a book about the *Pensées*. It will be a book about what the *Pensées* are about, a book that employs those notes for the purpose of thinking through again their tre-mendous subject matter, which is nothing less than the nature of faith, reason, and the meaning of life. I want to join Pascal in attempting to lay out some coordinates for thinking about these things and in trying to chart some appropriate paths to take with our lives in response to what we come to see.

A few facts about Pascal, however, facts about both his life and influence, will help us to approach a proper understanding of what he has to say. They will provide a helpful introduction to our conversation partner.

BLAISE PASCAL was born in 1623 in Clermont, a provincial capital city in France. Historians have described it as a typical medieval town scored by narrow streets filled with filth and water, a breeding ground for sickness and suffering. And there weren't many activities available in such a town for the maintenance of health. At a time, for instance, when on a daily basis people without modern bathroom conveniences emptied full chamber pots out their windows and into the streets in the early evening, an after-dinner walk was out of the question.

When he was three years old, the young Pascal's mother died, leaving behind her husband, little Blaise, and two daughters, one older and one younger than her son. Four years later, Pascal's father, Étienne, a lawyer and high-ranking civil servant, did something very rare for the time. He resigned his post to devote himself to raising and educating his children. An amateur mathematician and a man with a very lively mind, Étienne decided to move the family to Paris, which offered greater intellectual and cultural stimulation. Once in the big city, they lived life in the fast lane. They socialized with the nobility, the wealthy, the leading intellectuals of the day. Nowadays, if a family of great means is throwing a party and wants to guarantee its success, they might invite a few movie stars, some television people, a rock singer or two, and perhaps some faces that have graced the cover of *Sports Illustrated*. In those days, by contrast, a guest list for a really lively party had to include a few prominent mathematicians and a supporting cast of other intellectuals. Hard for us to imagine, but true. So

even on social occasions, the young Blaise would have en-
countered a world of ideas. His education was not restricted
just to school time.

But those times that were set aside for formal education at
home clearly had their effect. Étienne liked to take a problem-
oriented approach to teaching. He would set Blaise a problem to
be solved, and it was the student's task to tackle it with all his
ingenuity. It is said that as a child at the dinner table, Blaise once
noticed someone tap a dinner plate, attended to the sound that
was produced, and set off to investigate the phenomenon, tapping on everything in sight. He disappeared for a while and, to
the amazement of family and friends, wrote up a little essay on
vibration and sound. You never know what might be going on
in their little heads when children are drumming on the furni-
ture. Young Blaise was a curious lad who was encouraged to play
with things and ideas. It was no accident that such a background
produced an experimental scientist of the first rank.

Étienne had decided from the beginning to educate Blaise
in all major traditional subjects except for one. He believed
that there was one component of the curriculum that was just
too exciting for young boys, a subject far too intoxicating and
all-consuming to be taught to Blaise before the age of fifteen
or sixteen. Étienne was afraid that once he got a peek at it,
Blaise would become so entranced that he would neglect everything else. So this cautious father, this careful educator, went
to the trouble of hiding, in a locked closet, all of the math
books. For the protection of an impressionable young mind.
But one of his sisters tells us that at about the age of eleven,
Blaise was caught by his father out back of the house furtively
doing geometry. According to her reminiscences, he was in the
process of discovering much of Euclid for himself. The elder
mathematician was so overcome by joy that he immediately
unlocked all the math books and set his young prodigy free.

At the age of thirteen, Blaise was taken by his father to weekly discussion groups held at the homes of friends. Members of the intellectual circle attending these meetings included many of the greatest scientists, mathematicians, and lawyers of the day, such as Mersenne, Roberval, Gassendi, Petit, Le Pailleur, Fermat, and Desargues. The group had connections to such famous names as Hobbes and Descartes and was itself a hotbed of intellectual inquiry. Once a meeting began, one member of the group would make bold to present a thesis or a paper defending some new or controversial idea. He then became a target. All present would engage in a disputation and critical discussion of the proposition before them. An objection would be raised. It would be answered. A follow-up criticism would be lodged. A rejoinder would ensue. The give-and-take of lively and sometimes heated argument must have been quite impressive to the young adolescent who had come to watch and listen, because, decades later when he turned his talents to an investigation of religious belief, Pascal often would employ the device of an imaginary interlocutor, a sort of representative dialogue partner who would raise objections and ask penetrating questions in the same kind of dialectical give-and-take he had been exposed to in this high-powered discussion group. Everything to which he was exposed had its effect.

At the age of sixteen, Pascal presented his own paper on conic sections to the group. His work excited a great deal of admiration on the part of the older, established members of the group, and his talents soon became legendary. In fact, he began to enjoy so much attention and renown as to produce a good bit of jealousy on the part of some of the senior intellectuals ruling the roost who did not relish the competition and did not hesitate to express their pique. One particular scientist of the time characterized this upstart as "a young man with plenty of brains, but very ignorant." When he heard this,

Pascal replied, "There is a man for you who is terribly learned, but has hardly any brains."

Étienne, meanwhile, was caught up in a controversy of his own regarding government finances. He had invested money in government bonds, and the government had decided not to make payments due him and his fellow investors. They protested vigorously and, as a result, the elder Pascal had to leave town and go into hiding for a time. One of his daughters, having performed in a play before the powerful Cardinal Richelieu, pleaded for her father's safety and was granted her request. Richelieu even gave Étienne a gift. He put him in charge of imposing and collecting taxes in Upper Normandy, with all the financial benefits that involved. Of course, Upper Normandy had just been in armed and bloody revolt against taxes, so the new position was an interesting gift to receive, to say the least.

Yet, with military protection, Étienne set about his business with the aid of his son. Many nights Blaise sat up with his father until the early hours of the morning, calculating taxes. As they worked the long hours, they could hear the town clock in Rouen chiming the hour, one stroke after another. It occurred to Blaise that if the mechanism of the town clock could calculate the hour, they should be able to build a machine to do their mathematical calculations. With great enthusiasm, Étienne encouraged his son to pursue this idea. And over a period of two years, Blaise himself built more than fifty models of a calculating machine. This accomplishment in itself was, in those days, a marvel of engineering and craftsmanship at least as impressive as the development of the theory involved in the creation of the machine.

This whole episode highlights the many facets of Pascal's genius. One of his strengths in projective geometry was his vivid and concrete imagination. That imagination caught fire in this case and led to the physical production of a machine that has been recognized as a precursor of modern computers. Pascal was no mere thinker. He was a doer. Overseeing the construction of his machine was not the work of a pure theoretician. And when the calculator had been made, Pascal became a salesman. Foreseeing the potential market for devices such as this, he produced some promotional literature, which primarily took the form of a dialogue with a skeptical customer. Pascal presented his machine, raised objections, and laid out answers to those objections, echoing the dialectical give-and-take he had heard in his father's discussion groups from his early teens and anticipating the persuasive style of many passages in the *Pensées*. But Pascal realized that it would take more than intellectual argument to sell his machine. Human beings are not reasoning machines moved by argument alone. They have emotions and attitudes that must be moved and aesthetic sensibilities that must be taken into consideration. So Pascal hired a poet to write a promotional sonnet, a seventeenth-century version of an advertising jingle. Something a little more polished than "Sooner or later, you'll need a calculator," but a rhyme nonetheless.

He was a bit ahead of his time. There was not yet much of a market for business machines. And no way existed for building them in great numbers. But that was Pascal — blazing a path, imagining new things, pioneering innovative ways of thinking and doing. Later he produced important work on the question of whether a vacuum could exist in nature. Impatient with the purely speculative arguments of philosophers, he devised experiments following the work of Torricelli in Italy and thus demonstrated important truths about atmospheric pressure, results significant for the science of pneumatics. In a few more years, he became fascinated with games of chance and laid some of the foundations for probability theory and

that powerful science of calculation used by both nuclear strate-
gists and football coaches, modern decision theory. He also
designed the first system of public transportation in Europe.
From the highly abstract to the most mundane of matters, his
incisive mind was fertile soil for creative innovations both in
mathematics and in the sciences. And the same proclivities of
thought were at work when he turned his attention to matters
of religion and the human condition. A keen analytical ability,
a vivid concrete imagination, and a sense of the practical —
the value of *doing* as well as thinking — were his strengths, and
they produced powerful results in his work.

 A few words about the religious history of his family and
his own spiritual odyssey are in order. The Pascal clan was a
conventionally religious Catholic family. When Blaise was
about twenty-two or twenty-three, his father was involved in
an accident and had to call on a pair of bonesetters. The two
men, brothers, were followers of the religious thinker Cornelius
Jansen. Jansen had written a big book on Saint Augustine in
which he stressed the importance of the grace of God in the
economy of salvation and the necessity for living out one's faith
on a daily basis. One of Jansen's school friends, the Abbé de
Saint-Cyran, was a church reformer who wanted to put Jansen's
ideas into practice. He once said, "There has not been a *real*
church in five or six hundred years," thereby not exactly en-
dearing himself to a great many of his fellow churchmen.
Richelieu once said of Saint-Cyran that "His entrails are on fire
and they send into his head vapors which he mistakes for
inspiration" — one of the greatest put-downs of all time.

Pascal's involvement with Jansenism, which began with the
acquaintance of the two brothers, had a profound effect on
him. He underwent a sort of religious awakening. The melding
of the theoretical and practical in Jansenist teaching struck a
chord in him. Jansenism came to be considered in various ways

a Catholic heresy, a matter that was hotly debated at the time. Pascal entered the fray with brilliantly written letters attacking the Jesuits, the main adversaries of Jansenism. Written and printed in secret, these *Provincial Letters* were widely distributed and were immensely popular. Many students of French literature consider them to have set standards never surpassed for polemical prose style.

It is debated whether Pascal ever considered himself a Jansenist. He was certainly a friend to many leading Jansenists, and one of his sisters entered a Jansenist order. Involved as he was with them, and with their defense, he learned many fine points of theology and began to develop a new sense of the importance of the Christian faith for a meaningful human existence.

At the age of twenty-nine, after the death of his father, Pascal began what many historians refer to as his "worldly period." He immersed himself with gusto in the social life and entertainments of his friends for a period of about two years. Insights apparently gained during this time later played an important role in his diagnosis of the human condition that figures so powerfully in the *Pensées*. Then on the night of November 23, 1654, at the age of thirty-one, Pascal had a profound and deeply moving mystical experience that dramatically turned him around, reorienting all his priorities. This is referred to by biographers as "The Night of Fire," because an image or vision of fire seems to have figured prominently in what transpired.

There is no indication that Pascal ever mentioned this experience to anyone while he lived. It was only after he died that a servant discovered a record of the event sewn into the lining of his coat. Scientist that he was, even when he was having a sudden, unexpected mystical experience, an experience that would change his life, Pascal apparently had the presence of mind and inclination to take notes. Now the notes are, to be sure, a bit enigmatic, but they were important enough to him that he carefully copied them onto a piece of parchment and carried them with him secretly at all times for the rest of his life. They contain the only reference we have to an experience that set him on a course that consumed most of his energies for the rest of his days.

He conceived a project. He would write a book powerfully presenting the Christian faith to his unbelieving friends and contemporaries. He began taking notes, sketching arguments, outlining ideas. And then, before he could even begin to polish them into the flow of prose he envisioned, he weakened and died. A lifetime of sickness and suffering, which had never been able to block out the light of his genius, extinguished it from this earth in his thirty-ninth year: 1623-1662.

But the notes he had left behind were organized. At least, many were, grouped under headings, fastened together, ready for use. A few years after his death, a selection of the notes was published, and over the years various collections, arrangements, and editions have been put into print. The history of these versions is a long and tortuous one, outside the realm of our concern here. I'll be quoting from the Lafuma edition, as translated primarily by Alban Krailsheimer (*Pensées,* Penguin Classics Edition). The individual notes are numbered, and this numbering differs from that used in the older Brunsvig edition, which has also had its English translators.

Because of the nature of the text — it is a collection of notes for a book and not a book itself — the *Pensées* can be hard to read cover-to-cover. Brilliant insights flash from all directions, but there are also many passages that make many first-time readers wonder what in the world is going on. There are enigmatic references and incomplete thoughts. I won't be going through the *Pensées* front to back, commenting on the whole. What I want to do instead is to focus in on what I think are the most important ideas and themes to be found in or suggested by these notes, the main lines of Pascal's thought as I see it — the main coordinates on the map he has made to help us find our way in this life.

It should be no surprise that his thoughts on God and humanity have been controversial. Because of the way in which Pascal characterized the human condition, Voltaire called him "a sublime misanthrope," a hater of humanity. André Suares once said that Pascal, with God removed, is "the most accomplished of nihilists." And, echoing this, Lester Crocker once called one of the most perverse figures of history, the Marquis de Sade, "a Pascal without God." Even the prominent Catholic philosopher Jacques Maritain has decried what he saw as Pascal's "Christian cynicism."

But Pascal has also been called a holy man, a prophet, and one of our greatest religious authors. The Marxist writer Lucien Goldmann once dubbed him "the first modern man." Recognizing his importance, T. S. Eliot even went so far as to say that "Pascal is one of those writers who will be and who must be studied afresh by men in every generation" — a strong claim indeed. And in his recent best-selling book *The Closing of the American Mind*, Allan Bloom says,

> To overstate only a bit, there are two writers who between them shape and set the limits to the minds of educated Frenchmen. Every Frenchman is born, or at least early on becomes, Cartesian or Pascalian. (Something similar could be said about Shakespeare as educator of the English, Goethe of the Germans, and Dante and Machiavelli of the Italians.) Descartes and Pascal are national authors, and they tell the French people what their alternatives are, and afford a peculiar and powerful perspective on life's perennial problems.

Bloom goes on to misrepresent what the contrast is between these two great thinkers, but he is right that they represent two very different approaches to life and to making sense of it all. Descartes, "the father of modern philosophy," was overly confident about the power of human reason to discover and demonstrate the truth about every facet of life. Pascal saw into the troubled hearts of his fellow men and women and recognized the limits as well as the power of reason. Descartes was boundlessly optimistic about our power to understand and to prove *that* we understand. Pascal, by contrast, pointing out our weaknesses as well as our strengths, was bound to seem to some critics a pessimist, a cynic, or a nihilist — at least, it is no surprise that he would come across this way to anyone caught up in Descartes's dream.

Descartes is by all estimates the philosopher's philosopher, questioning, proving, systematizing. It is not so easy to categorize Pascal. What exactly was he? Well, he was certainly a mathematician and a scientist. He was an inventor. Was he also, as he is sometimes called, a religious mystic? A theologian? An early existentialist? Was he just a brilliant dilettante, a dabbler in everything? Some people venerate Pascal as a profound philosopher. Others say that, unlike Descartes, he wasn't really a philosopher at all, despite the fact that his *Pensées* and *Provincial Letters* often end up in the philosophy section of bookstores. After all, all sorts of craziness gets shelved under the heading of "philosophy" nowadays.

It's interesting to note what Pascal himself sometimes had to say about philosophy as a human attempt to speculatively discover, prove, and systematize all of the elements of ultimate truth by pure reason alone:

> Even if it were true we do not think that the whole of philosophy would be worth an hour's effort. (84)

and

> We always picture Plato and Aristotle wearing long academic
> gowns, but they were ordinary decent people like anyone else,
> who enjoyed having a laugh with their friends. And when
> they amused themselves by composing their *Laws* and *Politics*
> they did it for fun. It was the least serious and least philo-
> sophical part of their lives: the most philosophical part was
> living simply and without fuss. (533)

Finally, a remark beloved of logic students:

> It is amusing to think that there are people in the world who
> have renounced all the laws of God and nature only to invent
> laws for themselves, which they scrupulously obey, as, for
> example, Mahomet's soldiers, thieves and heretics, and
> likewise logicians. (794)

Pascal was certainly not slow to poke fun at some of the
philosophers known in his day and to deflate what he considered their pretentious and arrogant claims to ultimate knowledge.

However else Pascal should be categorized, it is safe to say
that he was a brilliant and profound Christian thinker who
exercised his considerable intellect in a number of fields and
that he has come to be known to history primarily as a person
who articulated the Christian vision of reality in an unusually
penetrating and insightful way. He shocks, he amuses, he
dazzles, he irritates, and he galvanizes his readers. Whether we
find ourselves arguing with him or cheering him on, we inevitably learn from him.

That's why we'll be using Pascal's notes as our primary
guide. We'll also consult and learn from many other fellow
explorers along the way, from the ancient Greeks to Tolstoy

and Woody Allen. We'll follow whatever leads seem promising in our quest to understand faith, reason, and the meaning of life. I'm confident that the guides we'll consult will help us along in our journey. They may not get us out of the woods altogether, but they'll get us moving in the right direction.

2

THE FOLLY OF INDIFFERENCE

To be utterly lost in the woods is unfortunate. To be absolutely unconcerned about it is unreasonable. Yet so many people who spend weeks mastering a new video game, months learning a tennis serve, or years perfecting a golf swing will not invest a few days, or even a matter of hours, in the effort to understand better some of the deeper questions about life. In Pascal's day, there were some intelligent and otherwise well-informed people who seemed totally apathetic about ultimate issues. In our day, there are a great many. With the book he planned to write, Pascal wanted to shock his indifferent friends out of their apathy and goad them into a philosophical and religious line of inquiry about life. His final goal was to lead them to see the truth of the Christian faith. But first, he had to get their attention. He had to show them that it was in their interest to listen. He had to make them care.

A teacher once asked a very bright but unmotivated student, "What's the difference between ignorance and indifference?" The student replied, "I don't know and I don't care." And that's exactly right. An ignorant person does not know, an indifferent person does not care. The ignorant person has not learned. The indifferent person will not learn — unless someone jump-starts his dead battery. Indifference, apathy, unconcern, and disdain are the greatest obstacles any teacher faces. If Pascal was to teach those who most needed to be taught, he had to do whatever he could to remove any such blockages to knowledge.

Commenting on some of his acquaintances who did not care to be bothered with ultimate issues, Pascal said,

> Those who do not love truth excuse themselves on the grounds that it is disputed and that very many people deny it. (176)

"Look," such people say, "philosophers have argued about the existence of God, whether we have souls, life after death, and what constitutes the ultimate good for centuries and centuries. They can't agree on anything. The theists, the believers in God, have their arguments *for* the existence of a God, the atheists have their own arguments *against* the existence of any such God, and the band plays on. What's the point of entering the fray? Where does it get anyone? Shouldn't the wise person just keep a cool head, stay out of such matters, and turn his attention to more practical concerns, to questions that can be settled, to issues that can be resolved? When it comes to these ultimate questions, what's the hope of finding out, and what difference does it make, anyway?"

Ultimate religious issues and basic philosophical questions are indeed disputed topics. That much is true. Universal agreement on such matters does not exist. But so what? Does it follow that we cannot possibly come to know the truth about these things? Not at all. Is it unlikely that we shall succeed? I don't see why. We'll just need to think hard and proceed carefully if we are to get at the truth about such matters. We are not guaranteed success. But neither is it certain that we will fail. We just need to try our very best to get at the truth. And surely these questions are worth our greatest efforts.

A man once said to me that he had been told all his life there were three topics that should not be talked about in polite company: Religion, Sex, and Politics. He then went on to add that the older he got, the more he came to realize that these were the only things worth talking about.

A realization that religious issues are disputed topics is one cause of religious indifference. It is a very widespread rationalization, or "excuse," for it. People "excuse themselves on the grounds that it is disputed." Pascal describes such people as individuals "who do not love truth," and this is a telling characterization. An object of love is not a matter for indifference. When you have it, you embrace it; when you lack it, you pursue it. People who are indifferent about ultimate questions neither embrace nor pursue the truth on these issues. At one point, commenting on what is arguably the most ultimate issue of all, Pascal says that

> there are only two classes of persons who can be called reasonable: those who serve God with all their heart because they know him and those who seek him with all their heart because they do not know him. (427)

And in another note, he draws out the categorization a bit further:

> There are only three sorts of people: those who have found God and serve him; those who are busy seeking him and have not found him; those who live without either seeking or finding him. The first are reasonable and happy, the last are foolish and unhappy, those in the middle are unhappy and reasonable. (160)

The search for truth on such ultimate issues may not always be pleasant, but it is a reasonable use of our time and efforts.

And it is, in fact, unreasonable not to seek such enlightenment. So why don't more people seek for the deepest truth? Well, as we have just noted, it can be an unpleasant task. It can be arduous. It can be frustrating.

Confronting ultimate questions can also be daunting. In the film *Hannah and Her Sisters,* the character played by Woody Allen tries to tell his Jewish parents that he has had difficulty with believing in the God of their faith. His mother won't hear such nonsense and locks herself in the bathroom. The confused young man shouts into the bathroom, "Well, if there's a God, then why is there so much evil in the world. Just on a simplistic level, why were there Nazis?" At this, his mother calls out from behind the bathroom door to her husband in the kitchen, "Tell him, Max." The father replies, "How the hell do I know why there were Nazis; I don't know how the can opener works."

Here we human beings are with our limited backgrounds, our limited experience, and nothing to rely on but those three-pound gelatinous chunks of meat we call brains, and we expect to understand the deepest mysteries of life? Some people find the whole idea a little overwhelming, and even presumptuous, if not plain preposterous.

Others are just of a more pragmatic cast of mind and are impatient with philosophical or theological inquiries. In my house, I have witnessed this conflict of temperament on occasion between my son and my daughter. At the age of eight, my daughter Sara was a no-nonsense, practical girl, a bit impatient at times with her younger brother Matthew, a six-year-old dreamer and thinker given to asking philosophical questions. One evening after playing a trivia game together, Matthew and I had gone into the kitchen to fix a snack. Sara was in the dining room already eating. Matthew suddenly looked up at me and said, "Dad, why don't they make a game with really hard questions, questions nobody can answer, like 'Why was

God not born?'" Overhearing this bit of theological inquiry
from the other room, Sara shot back, "Because he was always
there, stupid!" Matthew wrinkled up his face in a pensive,
somewhat frustrated way and confided to me in a lower voice,
"Sometimes I have trouble saying what I mean. I mean, How
did God *get* there?" To this, Sara responded with evident irritation, "He just showed up!"

Some people want to pursue philosophical and theological
lines of inquiry, others don't. Some have the patience for an
extended quest, others have what they consider to be more
important things to do. Both my children are thoughtful, reflective, and very intelligent. Sara just wasn't in the mood that
evening for philosophical discourse or theological inquiry.
Some people seem never to be in the mood. And that, according
to Pascal, is unreasonable.

There are people who avoid religious and philosophical
thinking out of fear. Often this is just fear of the unknown.
Others fear what they suspect to be true and wouldn't want to
face head-on. Some people can't stand to read about quantum
physics, cosmology, or even modern astronomy because of a
sense of disproportionality they find extremely unsettling. A
well-educated and intelligent person once said to me that she
can't bear to contemplate galactic distances or even the size of
our solar system. She prefers to view the blue sky as if it were
a nearby dome and chooses to block out any thoughts of what
is beyond. When confronted with philosophy and theology,
some people seem to experience a kindred sense of metaphysical
vertigo, a sort of queasiness in the contemplation of the vastly
different. For some, any question of religion threatens a loss of
control or a loss of the sense of control many of us like to think
of ourselves as having over our lives. Just as some atheists have
suggested that religious believers are simply people who have
a deep psychological need to think there is a benevolent and

powerful caretaker watching over the world, some theists have returned the compliment and suggested that unbelievers are people who have a deep psychological need to believe that they are utterly free to do whatever they want with their lives, that there is no higher authority, no moral governor of the universe to whom they are answerable. If you're afraid of what might be out there, you may not want to peek out from under the covers at all.

Of course, as Pascal understood, some people who seem not to care about matters of religion fear only the opinions of their fellows. They fear being thought weak, they dread being labeled "religious" or "superstitious," they want to court favor with those "worldly" individuals they admire for their success, fame, or rebellious outlook on life. Their apparent indifference is only pretense. They claim not to believe and not to care, but this is only posturing meant to create an image of self-assurance that will gain them acceptance. "They are people," Pascal says, "who have heard that it is good form to display such extravagance." But is this really the way to court favor among the worldly? Is any sensible person impressed to hear of someone that he holds no beliefs on ultimate issues, and that he could not possibly care less?

In his *Confession,* Leo Tolstoy recounted the excesses and immoralities of his early years:

> During this time I began to write out of vanity, self-interest, and pride. I did the same thing in my writing that I did in my life. In order to acquire the fame and money I was writing for, it was necessary to conceal what was good and to flaunt what was bad. And that is what I did. Time after time I would scheme in my writings to conceal under the mask of indifference and even pleasantry those yearnings for something good which gave meaning to my life. And I succeeded in this and was praised.

If Tolstoy's experience is any guide, the appearance of indifference can be admired. But should it be? Pascal points out
that it is a mistake to court esteem in this way, and Tolstoy
himself came to see it as deeply mistaken. We should not covet
the regard of anyone who would prize a lack of care about
ultimate truths and ultimate goods.

Is there a God or not? Is the most basic truth about ultimate
reality a personal truth, or is it an impersonal truth? Are human
persons small anomalies blindly thrown up by natural processes
for a temporary, transient existence in an otherwise hostile
universe, or could it be that we may have both eternal value
and everlasting existence? Pascal was concerned about people
who don't know and don't seek to know the truth on any such
matter and so often "excuse themselves on the grounds that it
is disputed," whatever the true cause or reason behind their
real or feigned indifference.

Disputed questions can be divided into two very different
categories. There are, first, what we can refer to as *existentially
peripheral disputed questions*. These are questions that may be
widely or hotly disputed but whose proper resolution is not
really crucial for my understanding of my life or for my living
of a good life. Answering them is peripheral to the core concerns
of what it means to exist in the world as a human being.
Consider the debate that once raged over whether Marcel Duchamp's famous urinal was art. I believe the story went something like this. Duchamp, a well-known avante-garde artist,
found a discarded urinal one day, signed a name to it with great
flourish (not his own, by the way, but 'R. Mutt'), and offered
it to the art world as a new work of art. Well, you can imagine
where most art galleries would be inclined to install it and what
many critics wanted to do to it. Was this piece of autographed
bathroom plumbing properly thought of as art just because an
artist said so? What is it to be a work of art? The arguments

and counterarguments flew. Many people, however, claimed not to know and not to care. And perhaps that's just fine. It won't affect my life one way or another how those disputed questions are answered. Regardless of whether I ever arrive at a precise definition of "art" or "work of art," my aesthetic experience will be just as rich. And the Duchamp furor was just a tempest in a teapot (or perhaps I should say "in a fur-lined teacup," in reference to another of his unusual artistic productions). I need not care about how it is to be resolved, or even whether it possibly can be. For any such existentially peripheral disputed question, indifference is an altogether acceptable and reasonable attitude.

But there is another category of disputed topics, a group of what we can call *existentially central disputed questions*. These are issues that are widely or hotly disputed among human beings and that matter a great deal to how we understand ourselves and our lives. Indifference concerning them is a different matter altogether. Let us see what Pascal has to say about what he considers to be an example of such a question, the issue of life after death.

The immortality of the soul is something of such vital importance to us, affecting us so deeply, that one must have lost all feeling not to care about knowing the facts of the matter. All our actions and thoughts must follow such different paths, according to whether there is hope of eternal blessings or not, that the only possible way of acting with sense and judgement is to decide our course in the light of this point, which ought to be our ultimate objective.

Thus our chief interest and chief duty is to seek enlightenment on this subject, on which all our conduct depends. And that is why, amongst those who are not convinced, I make an absolute distinction between those who strive with all their might to learn and those who live without troubling themselves or thinking about it. (427)

He goes on to comment about people who are indifferent concerning such an issue that

> This negligence in a matter where they themselves, their eternity, their all are at stake, fills me more with irritation than pity; it astounds and appals me; it seems quite monstrous to me. (427)

Some readers claim that they find these assertions offensive. Why should all our actions and thoughts follow such different paths depending upon whether "there is hope of eternal blessings or not"? Is Pascal suggesting that people will live morally and justly only if they believe that such conduct will receive everlasting reward? Even worse, is he suggesting that we ought to decide on this basis whether to live morally or not? He does say that "the only way of acting with sense and judgment is to decide our course in the light of this point," the issue of immortality. But isn't it just false that a belief in immortality is a necessary condition of moral living? There do seem to exist people who do not hold out any hope of an afterlife and who nonetheless live morally. And it seems false as well to think that believing in immortality is sufficient for behaving morally. There are people who anticipate an afterlife but perform pretty poorly in this life. And, worst of all, to advocate charting our course on the basis of some rewards-and-punishments scheme seems to amount to no more than the suggesting of an immoral basis for morality, pandering to nothing better than the crassest self-interest to motivate a way of life.

These are serious charges, but I think they are directed at a reading of Pascal that is not forced upon us. His elder contemporary Descartes had expressed the view that

since in this life there are often more rewards for vices than
for virtues, few would prefer what is right to what is useful,
if they neither feared God nor hoped for an after-life. *(Med-
itations)*

This observation does not make religious belief either a necessary or a sufficient condition for moral living. Nor does it
recommend a hope of reward or a fear of retribution as the
proper motivation for morality. It just reports on a connection
that has motivational impact. And that there is such a connection would be hard to deny. Yet we do not need to read the
passage from Pascal as recommending or even countenancing
a quid pro quo attitude toward moral behavior, an exchange
of value in which the human being engages in a certain form
of conduct in order to secure certain results in an afterlife and
to avoid others. A subtly different and more interesting reading
of the passage is possible.

On my preferred reading, Pascal is just applying here what
we can call the *Context Principle:* the appropriateness of a form
of behavior is always a function of its context. That is to say,
the reasonableness of an action, an activity, an attitude, an
emotion, or a line of thought, as well as its value, is always
determined, at least in part, by the nature of the context in
which it takes place. This is a principle endorsed by all civilized
people and inculcated in the very young, who early on learn
the difference between their indoor voices and their outdoor
voices. Pascal's friends, who would never be caught under-
dressed or overdressed for an occasion, were always acting in
accordance with this principle in their daily lives — except in
its most important application. They would attend carefully to
every context except the ultimate context. Surely, in accordance
with the Context Principle, it should make a significant difference whether we live, act, and think in a divinely created

universe and whether our actions are preparing us and others
for an eternal journey. Are the fruits of my efforts restricted to
the tight confines of this life? Or can I engage in truly long-
range planning? Am I preparing myself and others for literally
everlasting relationships, or are we just ships passing in what
is really the darkest of nights imaginable?

The question about the existence of God, likewise, is not
just a question about whether one more thing exists in the
inventory of reality. It is a question about the ultimate context
for everything else. The theist and the atheist should see *everything* differently. In the same way, the question about whether
there is life after death should not be just a question about
whether we are to expect one more segment of existence, however long, after bodily death. It should be viewed as a question
about the overall context for all our actions in this life. Will
we live forever or not? That should make a difference not just
for the future but for the present. And those who believe in an
afterlife do not, by virtue of their belief, devalue this life. Rather,
they embrace a larger context that infuses much greater value
into the small things of this life. This seems to be Pascal's basic
point.

Many reflective people have seen this connection. Alfred
Lord Tennyson once said,

If there is no immortality, I shall throw myself into the sea,

which I thought to be a very puzzling sentiment when I initially
came across it. I might have said, "If there is no immortality,
I shall stay away from the sea altogether, stay off airplanes, and
drive only under ideal road conditions." Throw myself into the
sea? No way. What could Tennyson possibly have been thinking? Well, two other quotations I later came across threw considerable light on this somewhat enigmatic passage. The

nineteenth-century English historian Henry Thomas Buckle at one point wrote,

> If immortality be untrue, it matters little whether anything else be true or not.

And we have from no less a world shaker than Bismarck the conclusion that

> Without the hope of an afterlife, this life is not even worth the effort of getting dressed in the morning.

Now, these are fairly extreme views. And they are by no means universal. But in our own day, the former Marxist writer Leszek Kolakowski has added his own assessment that

> If personal life is doomed to irreversible destruction, so are all the fruits of human creativity, whether material or spiritual, and it does not matter how long we, or our own performances, might last. There is little difference between the work of Giovanni Papini's imaginary sculptor carving his statues in smoke for a few seconds' duration, and Michelangelo's 'immortal' marbles. (Religion)

The question is one of permanence and meaning and value, objective eternal meaning and objective eternal value.

It has been pointed out by some philosophers that we can endow our activities with meaning either by valuing them in themselves or by valuing them as means to goals we value in themselves. But is such human valuation itself an empty gesture in an indifferent or even hostile universe? Anything properly placed in a valuational context thereby has some meaning. It is endowed with meaning. But do our lives themselves and our valuational activities have any meaning? The answer of the Judeo-Christian religious tradition is that they do. Our lives have a meaning that is both objective and permanent, transcending what we can now see, a value with which they are endowed by an eternally existent, absolutely perfect creator God. Much in life is up to us, but much is also provided. There are objective, proper goals for all human life and activity, moral and spiritual goals whose attainment is to issue in an everlasting fulfillment of intrinsic good. This is the message emphasized by Christian teaching, by the sort of teaching Pascal wanted to share with his indifferent contemporaries. Our little lives play themselves out in an infinite and eternal context, from which alone they can derive their deepest meanings. This is the urgent message Pascal wanted to convey. If it is true, it is a message we all need to hear.

I think that the Context Principle is beyond reproach. A very different application of it once was made by the philosopher Bertrand Russell, no friend of religion, who in his famous essay "A Free Man's Worship" wrote,

> That Man is the product of causes which had no prevision of the end they were achieving; that his origin, his growth, his hopes and fears, his love and beliefs, are but the outcomes of accidental collocations of atoms; that no fire, no heroism, no intensity of thought and feeling, can preserve individual life beyond the grave; that all the labours of the ages, all the devotion, all the inspiration, all the noonday brightness of human genius, are destined to extinction in the vast death of the solar system, and that the whole temple of Man's achievement must inevitably be buried beneath the debris of a universe in ruins — all these things, if not quite beyond dispute, are yet so nearly certain, that no philosophy which rejects them can hope to stand. Only within the scaffolding of these truths, only on the firm foundation of unyielding despair, can the soul's habitation henceforth be safely built. *(Why I Am Not a Christian)*

Russell is right that it is only within the scaffolding of ultimate truths that a viable view of life can be built. But, from a Pascalian point of view, he is just wrong about what those truths are. The undisputed point between Russell and Pascal is that those truths make a difference, a great difference. Is the Russellian, atheistic view of the universe correct, or is the Pascalian, religious view ultimately the better one to hold? Do we care? We had better care.

Pascal wanted to shock us into caring. So he provided an imaginatively vivid passage, depicting how life ought to look from an unbeliever's point of view:

> Imagine a number of men in chains, all under sentence of death, some of whom are each day butchered in the sight of the others; those remaining see their own condition in that of their fellows, and looking at each other with grief and despair await their turn. This is an image of the human condition. (434)

This passage has shocked many readers, and for the wrong reason. "How can Pascal, a Christian, say that *this* is an image of the human condition?" they ask, adding that "It is so grim." Such readers fail to realize that what Pascal is doing is holding a mirror up to the unbeliever. He is trying to portray, from his own point of view, how life should look from the unbeliever's perspective.

But Pascal's words can serve to shock in the way intended only if they don't present the unbeliever with his ordinary view of things. What's shocking about being reminded of what you ordinarily think about something? The point is that the unbeliever, the individual who does not believe in God and in everlasting communion with him, does not ordinarily think about what the world is really like from his own perspective. He *avoids* such ultimate issues.

If Pascal could wake up one indifferent unbeliever, would that single individual then be able to see his fellows looking at each other "with grief and despair"? No, because they would be filled with grief and despair only if *they* also looked reality straight in the face, from the vantage point of *their* beliefs, or, rather, their lack of any ultimate beliefs capable of giving hope to the human condition. And most unbelievers, unlike Russell, do not do this.

How do they manage it? How do most people without hope manage to avoid realizing that they are indeed without hope? Here we come to the heart of some of Pascal's greatest insights concerning human life, and to the topic of our next chapter.

3

THE DANGER OF DIVERSION

How do people manage to ignore the deepest and most important questions of life and death? Why don't people worry more about what this life, with all its problems, is all about? To these questions Pascal has an intriguing answer. People manage to put on the blinders, to avert their gaze from these ultimate issues, and to avoid facing their utter hopelessness by means of *diversion*.

> Being unable to cure death, wretchedness and ignorance, men have decided, in order to be happy, not to think about such things. (133)

But how do we see to it that we do not think about such things? Consider this long and astute passage:

> *Diversion.* From childhood on men are made responsible for the care of their honour, their property, their friends, and even of the property and honour of their friends; they are burdened with duties, language-training and exercises, and given to understand that they can never be happy unless their health, their honour, their fortune and those of their friends are in good shape, and that it needs only one thing to go wrong to

31

make them unhappy. So they are given responsibilities and duties which harass them from the first moment of each day. You will say that is an odd way to make them happy: what better means could one devise to make them unhappy? What could one do? You would only have to take away all their cares, and then they would see themselves and think about what they are, where they come from, and where they are going. That is why men cannot be too much occupied and distracted, and that is why, when they have been given so many things to do, if they have some time off they are advised to spend it on diversion and sport, and always to keep themselves occupied. (139)

This passage ends with a separate line that is often mistranslated in such a way that it sounds oddly and gratuitously misanthropic:

How hollow and foul is the heart of man!

A better rendering would be:

How hollow and full of trash is the heart of man!

Our lives are empty. We cannot face the vacuum. So we fill our lives up with junk, with trash, with refuse. Translating the original French even a little more literally, we are, according to Pascal, full of crap. And it's our fault. We divert ourselves from our real needs.

Toward the end of the movie *Manhattan*, Woody Allen's character is talking into a tape recorder, making notes. He lays out the idea for a story about

people in Manhattan who are constantly creating these real unnecessary neurotic problems for themselves 'cause it keeps them from dealing with more unsolvable, terrifying problems about the universe.

We invent little problems and hold them close, fixating on them to block us from seeing the bigger problems. And, Pascal says, we invent more pleasant things to concentrate on:

> The only good thing for men therefore is to be diverted from thinking of what they are, either by some occupation which takes their minds off it, or by some novel and agreeable passion which keeps them busy, like gambling, hunting, some absorbing show, in short by what is called diversion. (136)

He adds,

> That is why men are so fond of hustle and bustle; that is why prison is such a fearful punishment; that is why the pleasures of solitude are so incomprehensible. That, in fact, is the main joy of being a king, because people are continually trying to divert him and provide him every kind of pleasure. A king is surrounded by people whose only thought is to divert him and stop him thinking about himself, because, king though he is, he becomes unhappy as soon as he thinks about himself. (136)

Go ahead and give the gambler what he would win at the end of the day on the condition that he stays at home. Will you make him happy? Absolutely not, Pascal says. And it's not the rabbit he's chasing that the hunter wants, it's the chase itself.

In his *Confession*, mentioned in the previous chapter, Tolstoy speaks of this in connection with his marriage:

> The new circumstances of a happy family life completely diverted me from any search for the overall meaning of life. At that time my whole life was focussed on my family, my wife, my children, and thus on a concern for improving our way of life.

These are noble as well as pleasant concerns. But a certain

degree of absorption in them can prevent our engagement with other concerns that should not be ignored.

Billiards, tennis, golf, jogging, cards, football, basketball, baseball, soccer, volleyball, concerts, nightclubs, MTV, restaurants, cars, magazines, clothes, flirtation, courtship, small talk — these and a thousand other activities, or focal points of our attention, can be used to divert us from thinking about the ultimate issues of our lives. I believe Pascal would have nothing, in principle, against any of these things, with the possible exception of MTV (it is a bit hard to imagine Blaise on air guitar, flying on the wings of a heavy metal video). I happen to enjoy MTV sometimes, in small doses, but that's not the point. What is the point? Entertainment is fine. Relaxation is fine. And we sometimes need to be diverted from stresses at work and other serious concerns. So, what is Pascal against? What is wrong here? What is wrong is our *always* using such activities as diversions in such a way as to keep us from *ever* having to grapple with the big issues of life. Characterizing the unintended as well as the intended result of such diversion, Pascal said,

> We run heedlessly into the abyss after putting something in front of us to stop us seeing it. (166)

"Running heedlessly into the abyss." That could be a caption beneath many people's lives. We do not stop to think until it is a bit late. Philosophizing does go on in our world. Deep religious inquiry does take place, but more often in hospital rooms than in classrooms or living rooms. When crises arise, we philosophize. But that's not usually when we have the clearest heads for figuring things out. Disasters bring ultimate questions to our attention, but they most often put us into such an emotional state as to make clear thinking very difficult.

How many of us would think about going to a gas station only after the car stalled for lack of gas? And yet too many of us never stop to reflect on what is needful for a good life until it is too late.

Death is the abyss. We want desperately to avoid it. We want just as desperately to avoid thinking about it. We want to avoid having to wrestle with all the issues it raises. We try to do everything we can to create within us a sense that death is not near, that it can be ignored, that ultimate issues are mists far beyond the horizon.

At the end of my graduate training in philosophy, about 1980, I had a very interesting conversation with a young M.D., a pathologist. He and I had completed our educational preparation for our respective professions at Yale, and we were both entering the job market. He was going into hospital work, I was bound for the university classroom. In the course of the conversation, I asked him what starting salaries were like that year in pathology. He said, "Well, so far I've gotten six offers. The low end is ninety thousand, and the more attractive offers go to well over a hundred. What are the salaries like in philosophy?"

I told him, "The low end is nine or ten thousand, the high-end, more attractive offers top out at about sixteen." His mouth fell open, and he just stared for a few seconds.

"You mean nine to sixteen thousand dollars a *year?*"

I said, "That's right." His brow furrowed deeply, and he slowly shook his head.

"But we're both at *Yale,* and you work just as hard as I do!" He was perplexed, and even seemed offended at the apparent injustice.

Why do we pay medical doctors so much? Because we want them to keep death from our door. We want them to keep death and the troubling questions it raises as far away

from us as they can. We want this badly, and we're willing to
pay.

But have you noticed that we pay the best entertainers even
more, in fact, much more — the movie and television stars, the
sports heroes? Maybe it is because we know, deep down, that
the physicians will ultimately fail, and the entertainers keep us
from thinking about that. This could also explain why we pay
philosophers so little: they *make* us think about it!

In his book *Human Options,* the contemporary writer Nor-
man Cousins said,

> Our own age is not likely to be distinguished in history for
> the large numbers of people who insisted on finding the time
> to think. Plainly, this is not the Age of the Meditative Man.
> It is a sprinting, squinting, shoving age. Substitutes for repose
> are a billion dollar business. Almost daily, new antidotes for
> contemplation spring into being and leap out from store
> counters. Silence, already the world's most critical shortage,
> is in danger of becoming a nasty word. Modern man may or
> may not be obsolete, but he is certainly wired for sound and
> he twitches as naturally as he breathes.

Cousins is right, as anyone who has tried to carry on a serious
conversation with another person who is wearing headphones
and tapping his feet will recognize immediately.

We can understand the power and pervasiveness of diversion in human life much better if we look for a moment at one
particularly interesting feature of Pascal's vision of the world.
It is an idea that I have found to be extremely illuminating,
and even exciting for the way in which it helps to explain
human behavior and a wide range of human problems.

Pascal saw the world *hierarchically.* He thought of reality
as divided into various levels or orders. The three orders or
levels he discusses in the *Pensées* are

(3) The Spiritual Realm
(2) The Intellectual Realm
(1) The Physical Realm

The first and lowest order of reality is the physical realm. It is impossible to exist as a conscious, living human being in this world without being confronted by the physical realm of existence. This is the realm that gives rise to sense experience and provides the stage for bodily activity. The intellectual realm is one level higher. It is the domain of analytical thought and reasoning, the arena of the mind. The highest level is that of the spiritual realm. Access to this reality, or to this order of reality, comes through what Pascal metaphorically called "the heart." It is the realm of charity, piety, and true communion with God.

These levels of reality are distinguishable dimensions of human existence and activity. A full, complete human life will encompass, or partake of, all three realms. But this, unfortunately, is all too rare in human experience. It is more common for human beings to live predominantly on one or two levels, leaving out or minimizing the other dimension or dimensions of value and experience.

One of Pascal's most enigmatic, short notes consists of only three words:

Pious scholars rare.

As one looks around the academy, this seems true as a general observation. But what's it doing in the *Pensées?* Why does Pascal say it? I think it just illustrates what we can call *The Problem of Incompleteness* in human life.

What, after all, is a scholar? A scholar is a person who is unusually accomplished on one level of reality, in the intellectual realm. The danger associated with such accomplishment is that the scholar becomes so absorbed in that one level of reality, so fixated on that one dimension of human experience, that he can come to depreciate, ignore, or be altogether blind to some other equally real and valuable dimension of life. Isn't one of our best-known, most long-standing cultural caricatures that of the egghead, the intellectual nerd who can't find his way around properly in the physical world? The genius can't tie his shoes, never remembers where his car is parked, wears mismatched socks, and forgets that he already has seventeen ballpoint pens in his pocket protector. Admit it. We relish such stories.

I've been told by the friend of a friend of a great mathematician that this genius cannot remember where he lives, although his house is only a short distance from the campus of the university where he works. The story, sworn to be true, is that this man must count each day the number of streets away from campus, and the number of houses down the street on the right, as he walks home. Three streets down, take a right, twelve houses on the right. One day, I am told, as he was walking home he was deep in thought about a mathematical problem and lost count. Utterly confused and totally lost, he saw a little boy playing at the side of the road. He called out, "Young man, can you tell me where the mathematics professor lives?" The boy looked up and said, "What is wrong with you, Daddy?"

One more story. Another mathematician, this time the great Hungarian Eugene Wigner. I am told that Wigner was visiting one of our more prominent universities, and there was a graduate student in mathematics who very much wanted to meet him. But every time he saw the great Wigner in the math building, he lost his nerve. Why be so presumptuous as to disturb the great man when he may be occupied with some deep and important thought? One day, however, the young student saw Professor Wigner at the local post office. This was neutral ground. The great man could be approached. Summoning up his courage, the graduate student began to walk across the room, rehearsing how he would introduce himself to his idol. Halfway there, though, he slowed his pace and stopped. Wigner was grimacing with furrowed brow and beginning to slap himself on the forehead with the palm of his right hand, an envelope in his left. He began to pace quickly back and forth, apparently deep in tortured thought. Important theorems have been proved on the backs of envelopes. Perhaps a new proof was about to be born, or a whole realm of mathematics revolutionized. The grad student did not dare interrupt him, until he saw the professor become more and more desperate looking. Suddenly, our student forgot himself and blurted out, "May I be of assistance, Professor Wigner?" At that, the genius looked up, startled, and said, "Oh, yes, 'Wigner'!" scribbled the name onto the upper left corner of his envelope, and dropped it into the outgoing mail slot.

These stories may be hard to believe, but if you have any doubt, I recommend that you visit any major university campus, locate the math building, and go stand in the nearest parking lot at the end of the day. A few minutes of watching the mathematicians look for their cars is enough to convince any skeptic.

"Pious scholars rare." Pascal could have said, "Physically adept scholars rare." He also could have said, "Intellectual star athletes rare." For a star athlete is a person who is extraordinarily accomplished on the physical level of existence, a person with superb coordination and finely developed physical skills. It is relatively rare to find such a person who is also an intellectual. Why? Is there some direct connection between strength and stupidity? Absolutely not, although this seems to be a widespread belief. One of Aesop's fables, "Why Giants are Boobies," explains that there was only a certain exact measure of brains and intelligence available in this life for each person, a measure which is poured into each body by a god. Larger bodies get no more, and so the given allotment has to be stretched further and is not enough. Double the size of a man, and you get a half-wit.

But of course nothing even remotely like this is the truth. A star athlete is a person who devotes all his time and energy, typically, to the physical training necessary for his particular athletic excellence. And when he begins to win accolades, he can come to be so self-satisfied with his accomplishment on the physical level that he loses sight of the intellectual order altogether. What more is needed? He is a hero on his home turf. Will he hear the call from another realm?

A few months after I had been surprised with a teaching award at Notre Dame, I walked into an auditorium of three hundred freshmen on the first day of class and faced another surprise. There were more large bodies in the room than I had ever seen in one place. To my recollection, I had never had more than five or ten varsity athletes in a class. After the hour, out of curiosity, I telephoned the office that advises athletes and asked how many from varsity sports were in my philosophy class. The answer? Fifty-five. I was quite surprised and wondered aloud about whether I had somehow gotten a reputation that I didn't want, as an "easy" professor. I couldn't imagine how. I was reassured immediately that although not all schools do this, at Notre Dame the policy is to encourage the varsity athletes to take courses early on in their student careers with professors whose enthusiasm for the classroom has been recognized in some formal way by the university. The hope is that these faculty members will be able to excite all their charges about the world of ideas and that the athletes will

be led into getting as interested in their studies as they are in
their sports. On hearing of this policy, I replied, "Well, I'm
proud to be at a place that operates like that."

Of the twenty-nine freshman football players in that class,
twenty-six failed my first test. I called them together for a little
talk. "To play a game as complex as football at the level at which
you play it takes a great amount of natural intelligence," I said.
"You've mastered a tremendous complexity of subtle skills. That
shows me you're not only intelligent, you're teachable. And to
have risen to the top, you've had to be tremendously self-
disciplined. These three qualities — intelligence, teachability,
and self-discipline — are transferable qualities. They can be applied in any endeavor. They are all you need to do well in the
classroom. I am confident that you will not fail in philosophy. I
am confident that you will use these important qualities to
succeed at this task just as you have succeeded at others before."
And they did. There was spectacular improvement on the part of
these future philosophers of the NFL. They proved that a person
can ascend from self-satisfied complacency with excellence on
one level of reality to participation and fulfillment on a higher
level as well.

We've all heard of religious people who are so heaven-
oriented that they're no earthly good. Some approaches to
spirituality are notorious for disparaging the physical, for
waging war against the flesh. Nor is it so uncommon to find
in some religious circles a definite anti-intellectual bias. From
a Pascalian point of view, these are all distorted forms of spirituality. No level of experience should detract from the others;
to the contrary, each should enhance the others. The ideal
human life involves a functioning in, and an appreciation of,
all three spheres.

We have seen how an accomplished intellectual life can
result in a blindness to the spiritual or an awkwardness in the

physical realm. We have commented on the fact that a self-absorbed spirituality can become opposed to the body and the mind. And we have seen that striking proficiency in the physical domain can detract from one's appreciation of the intellectual realm of human experience. Understanding Pascal's three levels of reality can help us to understand so many problems of incompleteness in human life. Accomplishment on one level can block out the reality or importance of one or both of the others.

But often I have been asked why it is that so many highly skilled athletes tend to be very religious, or spiritually inclined. The cynic might comment that it's because they are not intellectual enough to appreciate the philosophical problems attending religious belief. As a philosopher, I don't think so. It is indeed noteworthy that so many good athletes have an active spiritual life, from the mystically inclined long-distance runner to the defensive lineman belonging to the Fellowship of Christian Athletes. Pious athletes are not as rare as pious scholars. What is the explanation for this?

There seem to be at least two or three different openings to the spiritual in sports. One answer to our question could be that people who are in touch with their bodies are people who are in touch with nature and that contact with nature conduces to spirituality, contact with the realm of nature's author. Second, there is something about team sports in particular that may have an effect. True team endeavor ideally generates some personal sense of humility, as the team player subordinates his desires, his needs, his ego to the good of the team. And, as we will see in more detail later, the state of humility is especially congenial to spiritual life.

There are two striking human passions, the passion for uniqueness and the passion for union. Each of us wants to be recognized as a unique member of the human race. We want to stand apart from the crowd in some way. We want our own dignity and value. But at the same time, we have a passion for union, for belonging, even for merging our identities into a greater unity in which we can have a place, a role, a value. That's one reason why we're patriotic, why we identify with our school or a church community, why we cheer on a particular football, basketball, or baseball team. We like to be proud of that greater community. But if we actually play on that team or if we are genuinely active in that community in such a way as to require the subordination of our selves to a joint endeavor we view as valuable, it is that subordination that can instill the real humility conducive to spirituality.

Whether an athlete is a team player or not, he is nearly guaranteed another experience that cultivates humility. As Joe Louis once said, "Everyone's got to figure to get beat sometime." Every athlete will eventually come up against his limits in an undeniable way. He'll see that he himself cannot guarantee the fulfillment of all his desires. Such an experience can open a person to recognizing a greater power, a power to be found in the spiritual realm. This, of course, is no sure thing. We can be self-absorbed in defeat as well as in victory. But there are aspects of athletic defeat, as well as facets of athletic victory and dimensions of athletic endeavor itself, that can bring us within hailing distance of spiritual insight if we allow them to. Unfortunately, we all too often do not allow them to. We use them very differently, in such a way that they become obstacles rather than avenues to the spiritual.

But how does all this relate to the power of diversion in human life? Very simply. Those activities that can absorb us on one level can thereby divert us powerfully from any participation on another level. Some of the most pervasive and potent diversions in our culture are activities in the physical realm that take our time, energy, and attention away from intellectual reflections and spiritual endeavors. But intellectual activities themselves can be powerfully diverting. Many philosophers and theologians are masters at keeping their distance from spiritual realities. A true grappling with spirit can be avoided by an absorbing intellectual gamesmanship.

It has often been noted that throughout human history atheism has been a predominantly urban phenomenon. Rural people tend to be more religiously inclined. Why is this? Is it because of the greater sophistication of urban populations? I think the explanation is much more interesting than anything like that. The city dweller lives in humanly designed and constructed places. He walks on sidewalks. He gets his water from the city water works, his light from the electric company, fuel from the gas company, food from the grocer. He is insulated in a web of human interdependency. It can seem to such a person that "man is the measure of all things," that humanity is self-sufficient, that his only dependencies are on other people and the products of their hands. The environment is, broadly speaking, one of human architecture, human constructs. The rural person, by contrast, lives in closer touch with nature, with its wonders and terrors, with the nonhuman, the greater-than-human. The country dweller lives at the edge of human control and is brought face-to-face with what is beyond our control on a regular basis. This conduces to a sort of human humility harder for the urbanite to attain. And it may allow for revelations hidden by the neon glare.

Intellectuals are prone to the same problem. The life of the mind is an interesting thing. One's thought world can come to be filled with human conceptual constructs that block out the light of the spiritual. The architecture of the mind can facilitate a better view of the world, or it can be used to divert us away from levels of reality not of our own making. For all the advantages the urban intellectual has, these disadvantages can be quite serious. It's not that there is anything inherently wrong with city life or with the intellectual elaboration of a human worldview, using the best of our conceptual tools. It's just that the activities of human construction, and the activities made possible by dwelling in human constructs, can easily become dangerous diversions — diverting us from what is most important in life.

Almost anything in this life can be used as a diversion. The category of "diversion" is a functional category. Almost any activity on one level of reality can be used to block one's awareness and appreciation of another level. It is because there are such distinct realities, or orders of reality, that diversion can have the impact it has on us human beings. Pascal rightly saw that we have to identify, understand, and control this force if we want to escape the indifference regarding ultimate matters that so easily, and otherwise inexplicably, engulfs us.

If we are lost in the woods, we must care about looking for a way out. Indifference is foolish. We need answers.

4

THE MEANING OF LIFE

ONE OF the most famous mid-life crises in history was the one experienced by the great novelist Leo Tolstoy. He had written such classics as *War and Peace* and *Anna Karenina.* He was very famous, celebrated by all. He was also rich. But in the midst of all this success, he suddenly found himself with a problem. In his *Confession,* written in 1879, he describes the celebrity, wealth, and activities he had been caught up in for quite some time and how he suddenly began to question the meaning of it all. He recounts the change:

> But five years ago something very strange began to happen to me. At first I began having moments of bewilderment, when my life would come to a halt, as if I did not know how to live or what to do; I would lose my presence of mind and fall into a state of depression. But this passed, and I continued to live as before. Then the moments of bewilderment recurred more frequently, and they always took the same form. Whenever my life would come to a halt, the questions would arise: Why? And what next?

He then comments,

At first I thought these were pointless and irrelevant questions. I thought that the answers to them were well known and that if I should ever want to resolve them, it would not be too hard for me; it was just that I could not be bothered with it now, but if I should take it upon myself, then I would find the answers. But the questions began to come up more and more frequently, and their demands to be answered became more and more urgent. And like points concentrated into one spot, these questions without answers came together to form a single black stain.

To do as he had been doing was no longer enough for Tolstoy. He had to know the reason, the real reason, the ultimate reason behind his doing as he did, behind his living as he lived. He had to know the point of it all. He found himself asking about the meaning of life. And his inability to answer these questions horrified him. At a certain point, he reports,

> I did not even want to discover truth anymore because I had guessed what it was. The truth was that life is meaningless.
>
> It was as though I had lived a little, wandered a little, until I came to the precipice, and I clearly saw that there was nothing ahead except ruin. And there was no stopping, no turning back, no closing my eyes so I would not see that there was nothing ahead except the deception of life and of happiness and the reality of suffering and death, of complete annihilation.

Simply put, Tolstoy hit bottom. And in this position, he says, his thoughts naturally turned to suicide:

> The horror of the darkness was too great, and I wanted to be free of it as quickly as possible by means of a rope or a bullet.

Many of us can appreciate Tolstoy's desire. At the age of

twenty-two, a young man once stood with the point of a large butcher knife resting against his stomach, both hands gripping the handle, resolved to plunge it in. He felt his life had already been disemboweled, so this was the proper end. He paused to review all his problems one last time, all at once. They seemed so overwhelming, so impossible, he suddenly became extremely curious to see how in the world they would play themselves out. He was completely intrigued. It was all too interesting, when he thought about it. At once, he realized he had to stick around, just to satisfy his tremendous curiosity about it all. So curiosity saved this cat. He put down the knife and fell to his knees. He breathed deep, and resolved to live. And, years later, he is certainly glad he did. Because his life has been immeasurably richer since the age of twenty-two than anything he could have imagined at that time. The problems that seemed so utterly overwhelming are now nothing more than vaporous mists in ancient history, long ago burned away by the midday sun.

An otherwise normal, healthy person contemplates suicide. Can it ever be rational for such a person to follow through? I think not. The finality of the act is incommensurate with the necessarily limited and incomplete perspective from which it is considered. Yet some people have thought that a philosophical argument in favor of suicide can be constructed by any person who comes to the conclusion that his life is meaningless, the conclusion that seemed to force itself upon Tolstoy. Let us, then, refer to it simply as *The Suicide Argument*. The argument goes roughly like this:

(1) I should rid the world of bad things, so far as it is in my power to do so.
(2) An utterly absurd, meaningless life is a bad thing.
(3) My life is utterly absurd and meaningless.

(4) It is within my power to rid the world of my life. Thus, (5) I should rid the world of my life.

This argument purports to show not only that suicide is right but even that it is obligatory for any person with an absurd, meaningless life.

The first step of the argument expresses a very general prima facie moral principle, which on reflection would be agreed to by most people. And its second step seems just as unobjectionable. Could anyone maintain with any plausibility that an absurd and meaningless life is a *good* thing? Nor would it seem to be of neutral value. Claim four of the argument is certainly true for most people, as long as there are knives, ropes, guns, and bullets around, high bridges, tall buildings, fast cars, and dangerous poisons. The form of the argument we are examining is logically valid — which is to say that *if* all its premises are true, it is such as to transfer that truth to its conclusion as well. It will follow from such an argument, as a matter of fact, that I should rid the world of my life, but only if it is true that my life is an absurd and meaningless thing. Tolstoy came to feel that his life was absurd and meaningless, and he felt a need to end it. He seemed to have thought that he should end it, in accordance with the conclusion of this sort of an argument. But he didn't. He couldn't. And that disgusted him a bit. Should it have? Not at all.

Tolstoy's inability to kill himself, I believe, resulted from a little common sense breaking through. How sure was he that his life was meaningless? How sure could anyone be of such a conclusion? A young man once thought his problems were unsolvable, and he was wrong. The judgment was made from an incomplete perspective under a cloud of disturbing emotions and pressures. How could anyone ever be so certain that his or her life was so absurd and utterly devoid of meaning as to justify undertaking the most final and irreversible earthly act possible? Perspectives can change. The results of a successful suicide can never change.

In the comedy *Love and Death,* Woody Allen makes a similar point. Consider the following exchange between his character, Boris, and Diane Keaton's character, Sonia:

> BORIS: Sonia, what if there is no God?
> SONIA: Boris Demitrovich, are you joking?
> BORIS: What if we're just a bunch of absurd people who are running around with no rhyme or reason.
> SONIA: But if there is no God, then life has no meaning. Why go on living? Why not just commit suicide?
> BORIS: Well, let's not get hysterical; I could be wrong. I'd hate to blow my brains out and then read in the papers they'd found something.

Philosophical perplexity can be a goad to action. But there are limits.

Why did Tolstoy think his life was meaningless? As we shall see, it had nothing to do with the peculiarities of his own life or life history. He drew that conclusion from features of his situation that are endemic to the human condition in general. That is to say, the features he believed his life to have, in virtue of which he judged it meaningless, were features he would have the same reason to believe true of every other person's life. But in that case our argument can support a further premise, which, along with its conclusion, we can call *The Ultimate Genocide Addendum:*

(6) Every human's life is utterly absurd and meaningless.

If Tolstoy, or anyone else, had good reasons, from altogether general considerations, to endorse the original premise (3), he would have the same reasons to endorse (6). But if these reasons are good ones, he could not avoid the even more dramatic conclusion

(7) I should rid the world of every human life,

as long as the power to do so was in his hands, or could be. Maybe this alone is reason enough to keep philosophy out of the hands of heads of state. Plato's ideal of a philosopher-king may not suit the nuclear age. Contrary to what we might otherwise have believed, it could be that arsenals of mass destruction are less dangerous in the hands of happy-go-lucky ex-Hollywood actors than in the control of brooding intellectuals!

To see how anyone could get into the position of thinking that his or her life — or everyone's life — is meaningless, we need to examine the question of meaning a bit further. We'll begin by getting just a little bit clearer on what Tolstoy's problem was.

Tolstoy believed he had some fundamental questions to which there were no satisfactory answers. At different points he expressed these questions a bit differently, for example:

> My question, the question that had brought me to the edge of suicide when I was fifty years old . . . is this: What will come of what I do today and tomorrow? What will come of my entire life?
>
> Expressed differently, the question may be: Why should I live? Why should I wish for anything or do anything? Or to put it still differently: Is there any meaning in my life that will not be destroyed by my inevitably approaching death.

Later, he says,

The question was: Why should I live? Or: Is there anything
real and imperishable that will come of my illusory and imperishable life? Or: What kind of meaning can my finite
existence have in this infinite universe?

And in one of his most powerful passages he explains that

> I could not attach a rational meaning to a single act in my
> entire life. The only thing that amazed me was how I had
> failed to realize this in the very beginning. All this had been
> common knowledge for so long. If not today, then tomorrow
> sickness and death will come (indeed, they were already ap-
> proaching) to everyone, to me, and nothing will remain ex-
> cept the stench and the worms. My deeds, whatever they may
> be, will be forgotten sooner or later, and I myself will be no
> more. Why then do anything? How can anyone fail to see
> this and live? That's what is amazing! It is possible to live only
> as long as life intoxicates us; once we are sober we cannot
> help seeing that it is all a delusion, a stupid delusion! Nor is
> there anything funny or witty about it; it is only cruel and
> stupid.

In Tolstoy's *Confession,* we find four topics interrelated:
(1) the reality of suffering, (2) the inevitability of death, (3) the
meaning of life, and (4) the existence of God, a subject that
comes to the fore later in the book, in Tolstoy's effort to grapple
with the other topics. To the extent that he is sure about
suffering and death and unsure about the existence of God, he
finds himself with a crisis about the meaning of life.

These are four topics interconnected in much great literature, and in other human art forms as well. A prominent
contemporary example of this is to be found in the films of
Woody Allen, which I have already cited. In *Annie Hall* the
young Alvie Singer, an elementary-school-age boy, is brought

to the doctor for depression. When asked what's wrong, he explains that the universe is expanding, and if the universe is expanding, one day it will all break apart. His mother adds that, as a result of this realization, he won't do his homework. "What's the point?" he asks.

In *Stardust Memories,* the filmmaker whom Woody Allen portrays is upset. He doesn't feel like making funny movies anymore. Talking to his business associates, he says, "Hey, did anybody read on the front page of the *Times* that matter is decaying? . . . The universe is breaking down. . . . Soon there's not going to be anything left. . . . There's not going to be any Beethoven or Shakespeare." He's overcome by the implications of these cosmic events. His coworkers respond by excusing themselves and, as they leave, telling him to have a nice weekend. He should go down to the beach. He should take a Valium.

In *Hannah and Her Sisters,* Mickey, again played by Woody Allen, was worried that he had cancer. When the doctor's report comes in, he is told that he's fine. After celebrating the good news, he is stopped in his tracks by a sudden realization that leads to a decision to quit his job and launch out into a philosophical and religious search. Explaining his decision to an associate, he says, "Do you realize what a thread we're all hanging by?" Reflecting on the inevitability of death in a way that echoes Tolstoy, he goes on to ask, "Can you understand how meaningless everything is? Everything. I gotta get some answers." Immediately he is involved in a search for God.

Now, what exactly is the connection among the four issues of suffering, death, meaning, and God? There obviously is a connection, or rather a set of connections, that brings these four issues together, but saying exactly what this connection amounts to is not easy.

Surely the enormity of human suffering is connected with

questions of meaning, because so much suffering seems entirely meaningless — totally senseless or utterly pointless. But why should the inevitability of death so often be the crucial factor in bringing people to ask whether life has any meaning? And what is the exact bridge to the question of whether there is a God?

Boiled down to their bare essentials, the reasoning presented by Tolstoy and so many of Woody Allen's characters seems to reduce to

> (1) Everything in this world will come to an end.
> So (2) My life will end.
> And (3) All the consequences of my life in this world will come to an end.
> Thus (4) My life is meaningless.
> And (5) So is everything else.

Many philosophers, however, have objected quite vigorously to this line of reasoning, asking what exactly the connection is supposed to be between temporal finitude and meaninglessness. Suppose there were no such thing as death. Suppose that everyone lived forever in this world of ours. What would follow from this (other than an unbelievable real estate boom)? Would the question of whether life has any meaning cease to arise? Of course not. We would still have the question of why anyone existed at all, and we would have the further question of what the meaning was, or could be, of this nonterminal infinite living. In this world that we actually live in, knowing of the inevitability of death does cause people to raise the question of the meaning of life. But a few thousand years in front of the TV set could easily have the same result.

We need some way of understanding the connection between death and meaning that does not imply that the absence of the former would leave the latter unquestioned. I believe such a perspective is available to us. It is a perspective that we can come to understand only after a few preliminary reflections on the nature of meaning. These will also lead us to see better the connection between concern over the meaning of life and questions about the existence of God. And seeing this will help us to appreciate more fully the importance of what Pascal has to say about Christian theism.

First, a general thesis about meaning. Let us call it *The Endowment Thesis:*

> Something has meaning if and only if it is endowed with meaning or significance by a purposive personal agent or group of such agents.

This seems to be a truth about meaning of any kind. Human languages provide the simplest and most straightforward example of this. No word in any human language carries its meaning as one of its intrinsic properties. No sound or shape essentially means whatever it does in fact mean when produced by a user of the English language as a meaningful linguistic utterance. And this is true even when the sound of a word seems to act as a constraint on what we can use it to mean, as in cases of onomatopoeia. It has been endowed with whatever meaning or meanings it has by linguistic convention, by agreement among speakers or users of the language. To have meaning of any kind, a thing must be brought under the governance of some kind of purposive intention, whether an intention to refer, to express, to convey, or to operate in the production of some acknowledged value. This is true of all meaning.

It follows from this that in any sense of the word "meaning," if anything in my life is to have meaning (or *a* meaning), it must be endowed with meaning. It must be *given* meaning.

Meaning is never intrinsic; it is always derivative. This is a point worth repeating: meaning is never intrinsic; it is always derivative. If my life itself is to have meaning (or *a* meaning), it thus must derive its meaning from some sort of purposive, intentional activity. It must be endowed with meaning.

With something like this in mind, many philosophers have suggested what we can call *The Do-It-Yourself Approach* to answering any question about the meaning of life. According to this approach, as it is often expressed, there is no "objective" meaning of life waiting to be discovered. To this extent, Tolstoy's negative judgment was right. But it is quite misleading to say so, because the life of any person can be meaningful to the extent that he or she gives it meaning. A person's life can thus have "subjective" meaning which is no less real. Insofar as we order the activities in our lives around things we desire, value, and enjoy, within the structure of goals we take for ourselves, we render them meaningful and thereby give meaning to the life they compose. This is the answer to the question about the meaning of life — so they say.

But is it an adequate answer? It certainly seems adequate to block the suicide argument, along with its genocide addendum. If human activities are meaningful to the extent that they are subsumed within the range of desires, values, enjoyments, and goals, then no normal human life will be utterly devoid of meaning. It's safe to suppose that some purposive structure is imposed upon the activities of any normal human being. And it does seem at least to some extent up to me as to how meaningful my life today will be. Will I lie around the house all day, sit in front of the TV in a stupor, or will I engage in activities pursuant to goals I have, values I recognize, or enjoyments I embrace? This is up to me.

But is the do-it-yourself answer all there is to be said? It seems to indicate that meaning is altogether subjective, that so long as some kind of structuring activity is going on in a life, that life has meaning. But surely there is more to be said than just this. It seems that it is just as possible to structure one's activities, and thus one's life, around trivial goals as it is to orient oneself around important, *meaningful* goals. How can the do-it-yourself approach account for this distinction? It seems that it cannot.

I have heard it said that all the questions about the meaning of life have one practical solution: find out what you can do well, and do it to the best of your ability. Focus your life on it. Then you'll find your meaning. But suppose Smith discovers that he's good at torturing people. Should he do it to the best of his ability? Should he focus his life on it? Of course not. To do so would be a monumental perversity. As an obsessed torturer, Smith would not serve as anyone's paradigm of a meaningful life. Likewise, consider someone who gears his whole life around a color, or a shape, or collecting matchbook covers. I'm not talking about a perfectly acceptable hobby but about a life-dominating goal or value. Such a person's life can be as fully structured as it's possible for a human life to be. Does that make it as meaningful as it could possibly be? Is there no difference between the meaning to be found, or the level of meaning to be found, in the life of the full-time, always on-call matchbook cover collector and the life of the devoted emergency-room physician or the life of the inner-city schoolteacher? Doesn't it make a difference *what* you orient your life around, what your values are? Surely it does. And it is extraordinarily difficult, if not impossible, for the do-it-yourself approach to acknowledge or account for these "objective" differences.

We encounter an even deeper problem if we adopt the do-it-yourself approach as our sole response to questions about the meaning of life. It arises in connection with an awkward truth about our ability to endow things with meaning. Let us call it *The Control Thesis:*

> We can endow with meaning only those things over which we have the requisite control.

I cannot decide right now that at noon tomorrow all the words in the French language will change meaning. I have no control over what any French word means. Likewise, I cannot endow with meaning any activity of a person on the other side of the globe or any person who has lived in a different century. I lack the requisite control in any such case. It is difficult to say just what kind of control would be required exactly, but I think there are plenty of instances in which we can recognize that we have it and plenty of cases in which we obviously do not. There are a few such cases that are particularly pertinent.

First, there is a lack of control of any kind over certain matters of personal origin that would be far too obvious to talk about if we weren't doing some philosophy. In philosophizing, it is sometimes important to dwell on the otherwise obvious, to see what surprises it may contain beneath the surface. The lack of control I allude to? No one has any control whatsoever over the basic circumstances of his or her birth. I didn't, and couldn't, pick the historical period, decade, year, or day of my birth. I had no control over what culture I was born into or what sort of social nexus I first entered. What would I be like now if I had not been born as an only child to loving parents in the state of North Carolina in 1952? It seems to me that my family background and regional origins contributed mightily to the person I am. What would I have been like had I been born in a very different cultural context, with a different language filtering and contributing to my experiences of the world? My personality and thought life might have been very different from what they are now. These particulars of origin over which I had no control have had a pronounced and determinative effect on the shape and direction of my life, on what values I have, and on what activities I pursue.

In addition, consider the many contingencies and vicissitudes of my life, my growth, development, and maturation, over which I have had no control. The sorts of people who lived in my neighborhood, the schools I attended, the people I met at those schools, the particular young woman I happened to be introduced to who became my wife, the specific sets of characteristics making my children the unique individuals they are, the many people who cross my path and enrich my life at the university and in the community — all these are matters over which, ultimately, I have had either absolutely no control or so little control as to be utterly insignificant. But these are many of the features of my life that have significantly influenced what I am like and what I do in this world. How exactly do I endow them with meaning?

Consider also the fact that I suffer. We all suffer. Do we have any control over whether we ever suffer or not? No. We have some degree of control over how we respond to our circumstances and over what circumstances we get ourselves into, and to that extent we have some degree of control, however small or potentially extensive, over how we suffer and how much we suffer. But it usually is very small indeed. And over the basic issue of whether suffering will ever darken our doors we have no say at all.

Finally, there is death. It is the ultimate instance of our lack of control. By risky or careful living, by suicide or by avoidance behavior, by the way we think and the way we act we have some measure of control over the circumstances and timing of our own deaths, but never complete control that can be used in any positive way. Never even enough such control. And as to the deeper issue of whether we will die or not, we there have absolutely no control. The rosiest prospects for longevity are severely circumscribed by basic unalterable facts about this universe of ours. As Woody Allen points out, the universe is expanding. Matter is decaying. Over this, and over our mortality, we have no control.

So what exactly is outside the scope of our control? Well, to put it bluntly, nothing more than birth, life, suffering, and death. And if all this is outside our control, we do not have the requisite control to see to it that our lives are completely meaningful, through and through, from first to last. We can create islands of meaning in this sea of existence we've been given, but it is beyond the power of any of us to endow with meaning the entirety of life itself or the entirety of any of our own lives. It seems that anything we build we will build with materials that have been given to us, and all of it will apparently be taken away by death — by the heat death of the universe if not just by our own little individual deaths. This is the ultimate limit the do-it-yourself approach breaks against. Unless there is something more.

If meaning is just a matter of endowment, then either there is ultimately no big-scale, objective, complete meaning to life, or to anyone's life taken in its entirety, or else there is some intelligent, purposive agent with sufficient power and control over all these things to be able to establish the elusive ultimate meaning that Tolstoy and Woody Allen and I and so many of us seem to desire. This is why the problem of the meaning of life naturally and inevitably leads to questions about the existence of God. It's why Tolstoy found himself seeking God. And it's why Woody Allen seems so plagued by religious questions that he cannot ignore. Throughout his many movies, his characters often attempt to satisfy themselves with some version of the do-it-yourself approach to the meaning of life, but the

5

SKEPTICISM, PROOF, AND THE GOOD LIFE

THEISTS are people who believe that there is a God. Christians are theists who claim that God has created us human beings to enjoy an everlasting relationship of love and communion with him and that he has made special provisions for our coming to know him in the life and death of Jesus the Christ. If these claims are true, then they are certainly among the most important truths we can come to know. But here a question can very naturally arise: If there is a God, and if there is life after death, then why can't these things be proved? Why can't they be demonstrated, settled once and for all? The more important a subject is, the more vital it is for us to govern our beliefs concerning it as carefully as possible. With trivial matters, we can act and think in accordance with appearances. In matters of great significance, we must dig deeper and form our own views more carefully. In the nineteenth century, the British mathematician W. K. Clifford wrote an essay entitled "The Ethics of Belief," in which he contended that

> It is always wrong, for anyone anywhere to believe anything without sufficient evidence.

It's natural to suppose that the more important a topic is, the higher our standards for sufficient evidence should be. If the existence of God and the immortality of the soul are of such singular and paramount importance, then shouldn't we demand for them the most conclusive proofs imaginable?

As a matter of fact, philosophers and theologians have attempted throughout the centuries to produce such proofs. Starting from premises (observations or ideas) that would be accepted by all fair-minded, rational people, they have tried to construct arguments for the existence of God and the immortality of the soul that would be convincing to all. This effort, which has come to be known as *natural theology*, has not succeeded in its intended purpose. Not all rational people have been convinced. No argument has come to light with the power required.

Now, this does not mean that none of the traditional arguments for the existence of God, for instance, is any good. It's just that they have not universally been judged compelling. The cosmological argument contends that the sheer existence of our universe, or of any universe at all composed of objects that could have failed to come into being, requires an explanation and that the only fully satisfactory explanation would have to postulate the existence of a God who himself necessarily exists. The teleological argument, sometimes known as "the argument from design," maintains that the nature and degree of order to be found in the universe cannot be explained fully unless we conclude that it is the product of an intelligent, powerful designer. The moral argument suggests that we cannot account for the objectivity of moral obligation and value without acknowledging the existence of an ultimate personal reality on which all else depends, a moral lawgiver or absolute source of moral valuation. The ontological argument attempts to show from the mere idea of God as the greatest possible being that there must be a God. And there have been many other metaphysical arguments — from the existence of causal activity in nature to a First Cause, from movement to a First Mover, from the objectivity of mathematics to a divinity in the numbers racket.

All these arguments have two connected features in common. Spelling any of them out completely — laying out all hidden assumptions, making clear all the inferential moves — results in a very complicated piece of reasoning. And, related to that, each of them has some feature, some assumption or procedure, some juncture at which it can be doubted. Remarking on such arguments as they come to be developed, Pascal wrote,

> The metaphysical proofs for the existence of God are so remote from human reasoning and so involved that they make little impact, and, even if they did help some people, it would only be for the moment during which they watched the demonstration, because an hour later they would be afraid they had made a mistake. (190)

And this didn't seem to bother Pascal at all. He had little use for these complex attempts to settle religious questions by means of pure reason alone. In another passage he said,

> Even if someone were convinced that the proportions between numbers are immaterial, eternal truths, depending on a first truth in which they subsist, called God, I should not consider that he had made much progress towards his salvation. (449)

But, as clever and even insightful as this remark is, it surely sounds a little too dismissive. Even if having a proof of the existence of God could not guarantee the salvation of our souls, or even get us very far down the road, wouldn't it at least contribute to the enlightenment of our minds? We can become troubled by our lack of any universally convincing proof, and we can find ourselves wondering why we suffer such a lack.

Some lines of explanation immediately suggest themselves. The most important issues we can raise are, almost by definition, the issues that connect up with most of the other questions regarding our lives and the world around us. Any attempt to settle such issues by reasoned argument, then, will inevitably become entangled with innumerable other considerations. The most persuasive lines of reasoning we ever come across are usually fairly simple trains of thought — which helps to explain why political debates so easily degenerate into the trading of short and snappy slogans. Conversely, complexity does indeed breed dubiety. Perhaps our most important questions, as broadly interrelated as they are with so many other issues, invariably, unavoidably generate complex arguments. And where ratiocinative complexity reigns, universal agreement is just not to be expected.

Maybe thinking about ultimate issues is also inevitably affected by how we react to life. Perhaps our emotions and our attitudes so color our basic perceptions of the world that we should no more expect all rational people to agree on ultimate issues than we should expect them to experience all the same emotions or have all the same attitudes. We often think and talk about human reason as if it were some utterly objective power we have for discovering truth. But perhaps the real truth about reason is not quite so flattering.

Human reason is just the power we have to organize and interpret our sense experience (what we see, hear, touch, taste, smell, or sense in any other way) as well as the power to draw conclusions that move beyond the confines of immediate experience. We sometimes talk of reason as if it were a separate organ for discovering truth. It is better thought of as a cluster of skills and abilities, abilities to work with and process what we're given as we make contact with the outside world and reflect on ourselves.

We like to think of human reason as a channel of discovery, a mode of access to truth, a fount of knowledge. We consider it desirable to be thought of as reasonable people. We want our actions and beliefs to be reasonable. We would prefer to reason through a problem than to fight over it. The historical period in which modern thought was born is often referred to as the Age of Reason. And many spokesmen for modernity have urged that every human problem can be solved, or every meaningful question answered, at least in principle, by means of a careful application of human reason or the reasoning process. The many astonishing advances to be found in the natural sciences and in human technology over the past hundred years stand as eloquent testimony to the power of reason appropriately employed.

But there also exists an ancient philosophical tradition that aims to draw our attention to the equally real limits of reason, a matter it is equally important to understand. This is the tradition of *skepticism*. The ancient skeptics, with the procedure they have bequeathed to us, have a lot to teach us about the limits of reason and the nature of proof. We can come to appreciate the insights of skepticism best, I think, if we dwell for a bit on what the original philosophers called "skeptics" were trying to accomplish, as well as on what exactly they did. This will best be done if we ruminate for a short while on what was traditionally the main quest of any philosopher.

Philosophy is, etymologically, "the love of" *(philo)*, "wisdom" *(sophia)*. Wisdom is, simply put, the knowledge of truths important to the living of a good life. In accordance with this, most of the ancient Greek thinkers we regard as philosophers were individuals who were seeking to determine how it is that human beings could live a good and happy life.

Anyone who thinks about this question long enough will come to an important realization. Our beliefs and our desires conspire together to produce the vast majority of our actions and our feelings. Whether I live a good life depends on what my actions are. Whether I live a happy life depends on what my emotions, or feelings, are. This is true for all of us. If you believe that in order for a person to be truly happy nowadays he needs to have a lot of money, you'll probably desire to have a lot of money. But if you also believe that you do not now have much money, you'll probably, as a result, feel frustrated and unhappy. Likewise, if you desire to be loved and appreciated by millions of people and believe that there are no millions of people doing any such thing, then you'll likely feel unfulfilled and gravely disappointed. But we don't have to put this on such a grand scale.

If I believe that a certain suit or sport coat would add great luster to my appearance, if I believe that a certain sporty red convertible would properly present my image to the world (say an Alfa Romeo Spyder with tan interior — you know the kind I mean), then I'll surely find deep within my breast a desire for these things. And my actions will follow along. I may make extra visits to the clothing store to try on that coat or hang around the Alfa Romeo dealership. I'll at least bring home all their full-color brochures and spend hours staring at those beautiful photographs of my dream machine. Is this the way to live the good life?

I may try to put together the money to purchase these things, even at some sacrifice. But chances are, if experience serves correctly here, after a few weeks in the new suit or a few months of zipping around town in the new car, I'll come to the realization — the altogether unwelcome belief — that these things have not fulfilled their promise to change my life after all. A certain small feeling of emptiness, or at least subtle disappointment, may ensue. But if from the start I have believed that I could not possibly afford these things, I'll just mope. Either way, my happiness is compromised.

If a person believes that lying is all right as long as it serves to help him attain his goals, he'll lie. Few people with any significant conception of goodness would consider such behavior part of living a good life. If a person believes on the contrary that lying is always wrong, he'll probably desire to avoid ever engaging in deception. But then, when he slips up and intentionally misleads someone, and so comes to believe that he has violated his own standards of integrity, then, once again, he'll probably be very unhappy. He'll have bad feelings about himself. Is chasing after career goals at any cost, pursuing attractive things, and seeking out beautiful people the way to live a good and happy life?

Some people think that the main human problem is personal unhappiness. And unhappiness, they say, results from the world's not satisfying our desires. They then go on to explain that there are basically two opposite possible strategies for resolving this disparity. Strategy number one is: conform the world to your desires. If you make the world be what you want it to be, there will be no room for unhappiness. This may be the preferred path of the ultimate Type-A personality, the aggressive world conqueror. It's not a very reasonable strategy to adopt.

Strategy number two is: conform your desires to the world. Stop wanting things this world is not going to provide you. That is the practical way of eliminating any gaps between your desires and the world. And without such a gap to enter, unhappiness cannot be your guest. But there is a small problem here. In order to employ this strategy, it is not enough merely to stop wanting things the world is not going to provide you. That can sound like reasonable enough advice; but even here, how are we supposed to be able to determine what the world is going to provide us *in the future?* In order, though, to erase all gaps between my desires and the world in this way, I would have to stop wanting anything the world is not providing for me *right now.* In other words, I can have what I want only if I just want what I have.

But what sort of desire would be left? What kind of desire is desire for what I already have? In line with the requirements of the strategy for avoiding unhappiness we are examining, I could not even desire to retain those things I now have — good health, a great family, a fine dog — because that would allow my desires to range beyond what the world is giving me *now* into the uncertain territory of what it may provide tomorrow, and this could set me up for unhappiness. But can I be said to have desires at all if they can't range beyond the present moment?

The Buddha took this a step further. If it is our desires that are at fault, if it is our desires that are responsible for our unhappiness, then the one guaranteed path for avoiding unhappiness and all the suffering it produces is to *cease having desires.* This is pretty radical surgery. But the Buddhist recommendation is based on the assessment that human unhappiness is a pretty radical problem.

Is it possible to extinguish all our desires? And even if it is possible, is it really desirable to do so? (Or should that be thought to be an inappropriate question?) In any case, it is not the only way to approach the problem.

Some Greek philosophers long ago came up with the subtle insight that unhappiness results not so much from a disparity between our desires and the world as from any gap between our desires and what we *believe* to be true about the world. If I desire to be loved by my wife and I am loved by her but I don't believe it, I'll be unhappy. Once we recognize this, we are presented with a third way out of our problem. We don't have to be world-beaters. And we need not snuff out all our desires. We can just suspend all our beliefs about the world. Cease to believe and be free! This could serve as a motto for a certain sort of skeptic. The original idea among the ancient Greek skeptic philosophers was that if we never trust appearances as reliable indicators of what is really true about the world, we will never have grounds for disappointment and thus we will never have cause for unhappiness.

Again, there is some insight buried deep within this wild recommendation. After all, isn't it quite common that the beliefs we have about upcoming procedures in the dentist's chair put us through a lot more suffering than the procedures themselves? I speak here from experience. For example, a couple of years ago I had some wisdom teeth removed. The very name of the procedure is enough to give any philosopher pause. And I have this policy never to have body parts removed without very good reason. So I worried. And my beliefs about the possible pain, and about prospects concerning the remotely possible, extraordinarily rare (but we've all heard the stories) fatal mistakes with anesthesia tortured me for days. By contrast, given the painkiller they did use, the procedure itself was a *very* pleasant experience. I'd do it any time. It was the most fun I've ever had at the dentist's. The point is that our subjective beliefs often inflict more suffering on us than anything in the objective, external world. And, the Greeks asked, how can anything make us suffer unless we believe we are being harmed? Cease to believe, and cease to suffer. Pain is one thing, suffering another.

But as a grand strategy for avoiding all unhappiness, this is even more radical than the Buddhist move. Our beliefs are typically much more extensive than our desires. Is it even possible to suspend all our beliefs about the world? And even if it is possible, could it ever be rational to do so? If it seems to me as if I am crossing the street too slowly to avoid the big truck that is bearing down on me, am I not to allow myself to really believe I am in imminent danger? This may be a way of avoiding unhappiness, but it also sounds like a way of avoiding longevity.

And, of course, some of the ancient Greek skeptics were legendary for never watching where they were walking and so for falling into ditches, walking into buildings, and that sort of thing. However, they were not all, in their own time, figures of fun. They were often revered for the heroic indifference they displayed toward life's apparent calamities. In the fourth century B.C., the philosopher Pyrrho, who is sometimes thought of as the founding father of skepticism, was given the exalted position of High Priest by his hometown of Ellis. And to further honor him, the city officially declared that philosophers would all thenceforth be completely exempt from any taxation. They would all have been made very happy by this declaration except for the fact that, of course, as skeptics they were unable to believe it was really true.

The early skeptic who was to have the most influence on subsequent thought was the Greek medical doctor Sextus Empiricus. Sextus believed that in human thinking on any topic there ought to be three stages of thought: (1) *antithesis* — a stage at which both sides of an issue are explored and appreciated, with contrary positions placed in opposition to one another; (2) *suspension of judgment* — a stage at which, having considered conflicting opinions, one withholds one's own judgment or belief, not favoring either opinion above another; and (3) *ataraxia* — the ultimate, desired state of tranquillity, equanimity, unperturbedness, apathy, which is supposed to result from not allowing one's belief to become entangled on any side of any issue. I say that Sextus *believed* this, but of course that would have been inappropriate. Following his own filmmaker himself seems haunted by its inadequacy and hounded by a need to seek the divine.

The fact of death, or the inevitability of death, does not itself create the problem of the meaning of life, in the sense that if we did not die the question would have no purchase on us. Death is just the most pressing and threatening of the many signs that we lack the control sufficient to be able ourselves to take care of all our needs for meaning. Only a being like God — a creator of all who could eventually, in the words of the New Testament, "work all things together for good" — only this sort of being could guarantee a completeness and permanency of meaning for human lives. As Tolstoy's case shows, questions about the meaning of life can be the most pressing questions we ever confront, when we break through the fog that diversions can lay over our lives. Such a breakthrough will send any person on a quest to understand. And the need to understand the meaning of life naturally leads to a search for God. The existence of God is thus no merely theoretical issue. It is an issue of the most ultimate personal importance.

advice, he should have suspended judgment on this whole business as well. But such was his advice, and, from what we know of him, it seems to have captured his practice. When asked how a wise man should live, having attained *ataraxia,* or the tranquillity of nonbelief, Sextus further advised that we should live in accordance with appearances (never, however, really taking them as realities), in response to our felt physical needs, and in deference to what the local laws seem to be. In all ways a wise person should avoid tension and conflict.

By the seventeenth century, Pascal's time, skepticism was again very much in the air. A number of developments in the previous century had resulted in this. There was, for example, in the early half of the sixteenth century, the work done by a great name among Renaissance philosophers, Henrickus Cornelius Agrippa Von Nettlesheim (not a particularly good philosopher, just a great name, though my personal favorites in this historical period are the names "Pietro Pomponazzi," "Pico della Mirandola," and "Pietro Bembo"). After lengthy study and reflection, Agrippa drew the conclusion that all human wisdom is just uncertainty and vanity. He also was one of the first big-name thinkers to point out that "philosophers disagree about everything." In the second half of the sixteenth century, the diligent scholar Francesco Sánchez summed up his arduous quest to delineate the scope of human learning and our capacity for truth with the surprising report that "Nothing is known."

The writings of Sextus Empiricus had been translated from Greek and were having their impact on the intellectual life of Europe. The most powerful adaptation of skeptical arguments and procedures was made by the great French essayist Michel de Montaigne, with whose work the century culminated. Montaigne was enormously influential and had a profound impact on Pascal. From Montaigne, Pascal came to appreciate the power and attraction of skeptical questioning. Pascal did not accept the skeptics' strategy for avoiding unhappiness, however. Recall that Buddhists maintain that having desires is the source of all our troubles. According to the skeptics, having beliefs is the problem. The Christian perspective represented by Pascal holds that it is not the mere having of desires and beliefs that leads to unhappiness but rather having *false* beliefs on matters important for the living of a good life and having *unruly* desires that robs us of true happiness. The solution is not to get rid of all desire or all belief. That would be throwing out the baby with the bathwater if anything is. The solution is rather to gain genuine wisdom, uprooting false belief and replacing it with true insights and perspectives, and along with that to gain some measure of control over one's desires. To live a good and happy life it is necessary to know some important truths about what is good and to have desires that are consonant with those truths. When the quest to avoid unhappiness eclipses or is confused with the need for true happiness or the need for a good life, inappropriate and extreme strategies for living are bound to result. And a false diagnosis almost always results in the wrong treatment. If our goal is to lead a truly happy life and a good life, we'll need reliable beliefs to steer by, and, like heat-seeking missiles, we'll need accurate value-seeking desires to determine our trajectory.

So Pascal was not about to adopt skepticism as what we often call "a philosophy of life," but he saw important insights to be gained about the human condition from the deepest probings of ancient skepticism, insights that will help us to get our bearings and gain some needed perspective as we attempt to tackle some of the most difficult of life's questions.

The Greek verb from which our word "skeptic" ultimately derives meant, literally, "to inquire." In the strictest etymological sense, skeptics are just fundamental and persistent inquirers or questioners. The skeptic asks probing questions about the status of our most common and basic beliefs — questions that we find to our surprise we cannot answer. Our inability to answer the skeptic can even be a cause of confusion and dismay until we fully understand what can be learned from this deepest of all probing.

Our main mode of contact with the world around us is through sense experience. But how do we know when we can trust the senses? The ancient skeptics gloried in recounting ways in which the senses can fail us, yielding unreliable information about the world. Sickness, or any other form of abnormal body chemistry, can distort the way we perceive. One of the clearest examples of this is found in the way food tastes. What is the right physical condition for perceiving accurately? How can we be sure we're in it now, or at any other time? For any such judgment will itself be the result of perceptions that may be delusory — if the well is tainted, the water will be bad.

And each of us perceives the world from a limited perspective. How can we be sure distortions do not result from the peculiarities of the perspective we have? And even if the data, or information, reaching us through our senses is accurate in itself, how do we know it is complete enough to give us, overall, a reliable picture of what is being perceived? The ancients loved to point out that many animals seem to pick up sensory information through more sensitive senses of smell, hearing, and sight. And as we now realize, our sensory apparatus is even more radically incomplete. The little bat seems to have a sonar capability we entirely lack. Perhaps there are other forms of perception possible, and even enjoyed by other creatures in our universe, of which we have no conception whatsoever. As some recent theorists have pointed out, the entire physical universe can be viewed as composed of vibratory wavelengths of information. The problem is that nature is broadcasting on all bands, shortwave, AM and FM, and we have our small receivers tuned in to only one frequency.

And what of reason — the interpretive and inferential processes we perform upon the sensory data we do receive? Severe sickness can shut down our abilities to think. And even small distractions can unhinge reason. Pascal lampoons the arrogant, self-assured man of rationality:

> The mind of this supreme judge of the world is not so independent as to be impervious to whatever din may be going on near by. It does not take a cannon's roar to arrest his thoughts; the noise of a weathercock or a pulley will do. Do not be surprised if his reasoning is not too sound at the moment, there is a fly buzzing round his ears; that is enough to render him incapable of giving good advice. (48)

And, again, he imagines the case of an individual revered for his perspicacity and judicious reactions:

> Would you say that this magistrate, whose venerable age commands universal respect, is ruled by pure, sublime reason, and judges things as they really are, without paying heed to the trivial circumstances which offend only the imagination of weaker men? See him go to hear a sermon in a spirit of pious zeal, the soundness of his judgement strengthened by the ardour of his charity, ready to listen with exemplary respect. If, when the preacher appears, it turns out that nature has given him a hoarse voice and an odd sort of face, that his barber has shaved him badly and he happens not to be too clean either, then, whatever great truths he may announce, I wager that our senator will not be able to keep a straight face. (44)

Any number of prejudices can bollix the functions of our reason. As any proofreader or editor knows, we most often see only what we expect to see. An education can correct our prejudices, or it can just instill in us new prejudices. And one of the most powerful forces that can act to undermine reason is the imagination. Pascal goes so far as to call it "the dominant faculty" in human life.

> Who dispenses reputation? Who makes us respect and revere persons, works, laws, the great? Who but this faculty of imagination. (44)

He claims that, as the dominant faculty, our imaginations are the greatest source of falsehood with which we have to contend.

> I am not speaking of fools, but of the wisest men, amongst whom imagination is best entitled to persuade. Reason may object in vain, it cannot fix the price of things. (44)

Albert Einstein once claimed that "imagination is more important than knowledge." It has great power for good. And, correspondingly, it has great power to deceive. In fact, this seems to be just one more instance of a striking general truth about this world in which we live, a truth that can be expressed quite simply in what we can call *The Double Power Principle:* "The greater a power anything has for good, the greater the power it also correspondingly has for evil." Examples abound. Often cited is the example of our harnessing of nuclear energy, with its associated contrast of nuclear medicine and nuclear warheads. Consider the more basic example of industrialization, with its tremendous profusion of technological advances, with all their attendant benefits, and both the environmental disasters and social deteriorations that we are only now beginning to discern as its accompaniments. Another more fundamental example would be the phenomenon of human desire. Without it, there would be no civilization, no culture, and probably no ongoing existence of the human species. But along with its glories, consider how many of the evils of history are directly or indirectly attributable to inordinate desire running out of control. Imagination is one of these great powers. It can motivate and focus the operations of reason like no other power. Its value can be tremendous. Or it can be one of the deepest, most insidious sources of error with which we must contend. "Put the world's greatest philosopher on a plank that is wider than need be," Pascal comments; "if there is a precipice below, although his reason may convince him that he is safe, his imagination will prevail." He adds that "many could not even stand the thought of it without going pale and breaking into sweat" (44).

How do we know when we are free of all these distorting forces that subvert reason? How *can* we know when we are? Or even more problematically: How can we know that we *ever* are?

This last question leads us right to the heart of the greatest sort of challenge that can be posed by skeptical questioning. And it is this challenge that will lead us into some deep and important realizations about the nature of our knowledge and the limits of human reason.

We form our beliefs about the world in many ways, directly from sense experience, from the testimony of others, from memory, and from various inferential processes of reasoning operating upon what has been given to us by sense experience, testimony, and memory. Let us refer to all of these as our *belief-forming processes.* The ultimate skeptical question can now be formulated quite simply: How do we know that *any* of our belief-forming processes are *ever* reliable? And the surprising realization that we quickly come to upon considering this question is that any attempt to justify our ever relying on any of our belief-forming processes, any argument or marshaling of evidence in the attempt to support the fundamental belief we all have that these processes are sometimes reliable will itself necessarily involve our relying on some of those processes (memory, reasoning, etc.) and thus will involve our assuming already the truth of precisely what we are being asked to justify.

For example, how do I know that any instance of human sense experience is ever reliable? The only methods I have available for ever certifying any sense experience at all as veridical involve relying upon the deliverances of other sense experiences. Suppose I try to answer the skeptic as follows: "Look, many times I have experienced something like this: I'm walking along and think I see a penny lying beside the road. I stop, look again, and find that I was right; it *is* a penny. I then bend over, pick it up and examine it more closely. Yes, indeed, a penny. My first visual experience, the initial glance, proved to be correct. In this and thousands of other ways I have found on a great number of occasions that my sense experiences are reliable. So I know on the basis of ample evidence that human sense experience is sometimes reliable." If I tried to answer the skeptic like this, I would be engaging in what logicians call "circular reasoning" — the evidence that I am presenting for the reliability of sense experience presupposes the truth of the very belief it is meant to support, from which it follows that the so-called "evidence" is tainted, and thus is no good evidence at all.

In a very short note enigmatic to most readers, Pascal writes,

Memory is necessary for all the operations of reason. (651)

And this is so. Unless we could trust our memories, we could never reason at all. In any inference, we must remember our premises on our way to the conclusion. But how do we know that human memory is *ever* reliable? Again, if we think about it long and hard enough, we discover that we cannot formulate a single noncircular argument for the belief that human memory is *ever* reliable. It's not merely that we cannot *prove* the truth of this belief that all sane and rational people hold — and must hold if they are to justify any of our other beliefs; it's that we cannot produce a single shred of untainted evidence in favor of this crucial and basic belief. What a surprising realization!

Descartes, Pascal's older contemporary, is well known for having pressed the skeptical question: "How do I know that I am not now dreaming?" I believe that I am not now dreaming, I think I know that I am not, but when I try to prove it, I fail miserably. In our own century, Bertrand Russell once asked how we know the following hypothesis to be false: "The entire universe sprang into existence five minutes ago, exactly the way it then was, with all its appearances of age." We all believe that this hypothesis is false. All our beliefs about things that we think happened more than five minutes ago presuppose its falsehood. Yet, again, we cannot prove that it's false. Nor can we produce a single shred of good evidence against it.

Deep skeptical questioning reveals that at the foundations of all our beliefs are numerous convictions for which we have no theoretical proofs and no good, independent evidence. A few examples would be:

(1) Human belief-forming processes are sometimes reliable.
(2) Sense experience is sometimes reliable.
(3) Memory is sometimes reliable.
(4) The world has existed for more than five minutes.
(5) There is an external world.

These are propositions that all rational people believe, and believe without any sort of proof. There exists no "sufficient evidence" for them. And yet they are vital, "framework convictions." They provide a framework of convictions necessary for gathering any kind of evidence for all sorts of other less fundamental propositions. These basic propositions are the fundamental assumptions of reason that reason itself cannot guarantee or even certify.

Pascal says,

> Reason's last step is the recognition that there are an infinite number of things which are beyond it. It is merely feeble if it does not go as far as to realize that.
>
> If natural things are beyond it, what are we to say about supernatural things? (188)

He adds that

> There is nothing so consistent with reason as this denial of reason. (182)

W. K. Clifford's demand that we have evidence for everything we believe is thus an impossible demand. There are beliefs it is reasonable to have, and there are even beliefs that it would be unreasonable not to have but that nonetheless elude any support reason can provide.

Pascal would have us part company with Clifford and with philosophers like him who believe that truth and proof must go hand in hand. But Pascal was no irrationalist. He writes,

> Two excesses: to exclude reason, to admit nothing but reason. (183)

In another note he says succinctly,

> Submission and use of reason; that is what makes true Christianity. (167)

On this topic he elaborates:

> *Submission.* One must know when it is right to doubt, to
> affirm, to submit. Anyone who does otherwise does not un-
> derstand the force of reason. Some men run counter to these
> three principles, either affirming that everything can be
> proved, because they know nothing about proof, or doubting
> everything, because they do not know when to submit, or
> always submitting, because they do not know when judge-
> ment is called for. (170)

Many of those propositions to which we rightly submit Pascal
calls "first principles." If there is no convincing proof possible
for the truth of first principles, and if "sufficient evidence" is
not available to show us they are true, how then do we come
to believe them?

Pascal says in a note,

> *Instinct, reason.* We have an incapacity for proving anything
> which no amount of dogmatism can overcome.
> We have an idea of truth which no amount of skepticism
> can overcome. (406)

The idea of truth we have is a deliverance of *instinct,* of *intuition.* We are given it. We are given first principles. We receive
them at a level of our being that is prior to, deeper than, the
operations of reason. This core of our being Pascal calls "the
heart":

> We know the truth not only through our reason but also
> through our heart. It is through the latter that we know first
> principles, and reason, which has nothing to do with it, tries
> in vain to refute them. The skeptics have no other object than
> that, and they work at it to no purpose. We know that we
> are not dreaming, but, however unable we may be to prove

it rationally, our inability proves nothing but the weakness of our reason, and not the uncertainty of all our knowledge, as they maintain. . . .

Our inability must therefore serve only to humble reason, which would like to be the judge of everything, but not to confute our certainty. As if reason were the only way we could learn! (110)

There are deep channels to truth available to human beings. But not all fundamental truth is always able to flow freely along these channels. Not all the basic truth we need reaches us. Sometimes the channels of instinct and intuition, the capacities of the heart, are blocked or obstructed. On some ultimate questions, reason may not supply an answer, and instinct may be perplexingly silent. We may have to take measures to get at the truth that are not quite as straightforward as searching for an argument or just considering the evidence. When it comes to the most fundamental things in life, the name of the game is not just reasoning. What then is it? In order to see, let's focus on the most ultimate philosophical and religious issue.

6

THE HIDDEN GOD

W HEN I was just a callow youth, I listened to strangers talk of their problems: angry tirades on this world's injustice, sorrowful tales of sin and despair, puzzled queries about life and death. Curiosity, grief, irritation and hate. It was the summer after my freshman year at the University of North Carolina, Chapel Hill, and I was living at Myrtle Beach, South Carolina, in a house near the ocean with thirty-some others, two to a bed, sixteen to a bath, not counting the roaches. During the day, on the beach, we approached people to talk about God and life and sin and salvation. We spread the gospel as they spread beach towels and lotion and arms and legs and picnic lunches. We asked questions and we tried to answer a great many more. I hated the thought of approaching a stranger and engaging him in dialogue about religious belief when he would rather be reading or swimming or just lying in the sun. But I did. And once the conversations began, I learned. Over and over I kept hearing the same question, or echoes of that question, really a challenge: "If there is a God, then *why* is he so *hidden?*" "If we have a creator who cares so much about us, why doesn't he *show* himself?" "Why is it all such a guessing

85

game?" "Why aren't the answers more *obvious?*" "How can this darkness possibly be *fair?*"

In a recent book, *Experience, Explanation and Faith,* the British philosopher Anthony O'Hear suggests that traditional belief in God faces a serious problem of rational implausibility. In a passage late in the book where he starts to lay out exactly what he takes that difficulty primarily to be, O'Hear says,

> A striking and surprisingly little stressed aspect of the whole problem is the way God fails to manifest himself in the world.

It's quite common to hear critics of religion say something like this: "If *I* were God, I'd open the sky over New York City, and in the midst of the most dazzling revelation imaginable, announce to the world that I truly do exist — the guessing game is over." I personally have heard a number of people say exactly this, with conviction, and no little irritation.

Of course, many times these are people who don't have a clue as to what exactly they would do about the most pressing problems of their own city if they were mayor, or concerning the greatest difficulty faced by their state if they were governor. They would probably be quite hesitant if asked how precisely they would solve the greatest national crises if they were president, but they have no hesitation whatsoever in venturing to declare how they would solve what may be the single most troubling cosmic religious problem if they were God. This irony of disproportion, however, may be a matter of appearance only. For it may be that there is a straightforward simplicity about the religious problem that is not characteristic of the lower-scale apparent analogies to it.

If there is a God who is the perfectly good and loving creator of all, it seems to follow that he would want the best for all his creatures, including his human creatures. At least it clearly seems to follow that he would desire the fulfillment and flourishing of all his creations capable of conscious experience. If, as theists typically claim, we human beings were brought into existence for the purpose of living in eternal communion with God, it would seem that such a creator would certainly do anything necessary to prevent our being in doubt concerning his very existence. To place us, or to allow us to remain, in a religiously ambiguous environment would not appear to be a loving act on the part of the deity. On the contrary, we would expect such a being to do anything possible to alleviate that most troubling of doubts created by the state of affairs religious people label "the hiddenness of God." In other words, we are tempted to think that if we were in the position of such a creator, we would do whatever was necessary, including celestial fireworks over New York City, to disambiguate the world and make clear to all rational creatures here below the ultimate truth about reality.

This is a powerful line of thought, and it does present a pressing problem for religious belief, a problem felt throughout the ages by sensitive religious people. Consider for example the writings of the twelfth-century Christian theologian St. Anselm, whom many philosophers view as the ultimate example of theological triumphalism, the religious thinker who claimed to have logical certainties concerning the existence of God. Toward the beginning of his book *Proslogion,* we find the following extended lament:

> Lord, if thou art not here, where shall I seek thee, being absent? But if thou art everywhere, why do I not see thee present? Truly thou dwellest in unapproachable light. But where is unapproachable light, or how shall I come to it? Or who shall lead me to that light and into it, that I may see thee in it? Again, by what marks, under what form, shall I

seek thee? I have never seen thee, O Lord my God; I do not know thy form. What, O most high Lord, shall this man do, an exile far from thee? What shall thy servant do, anxious in his love of thee, and cast out afar from thy face? He pants to see thee, and thy face is too far from him. He longs to come to thee, and thy dwelling place is inaccessible. He is eager to find thee, and knows not thy place. He desires to seek thee, and does not know thy face. Lord, thou art my God, and thou art my Lord, and never have I seen thee. It is thou that hast made me, and hast made me anew, and hast bestowed upon me all the blessings I enjoy; and not yet do I know thee. Finally, I was created to see thee and not yet have I done that for which I was made.

A bit later, in speaking about God, Anselm says,

Why did he shut us away from the light, and cover us over with darkness? . . . From a native country into exile, from the vision of God into our present blindness, from the joy of immortality into the bitterness and horror of death. Miserable exchange of how great a good, for how great an evil! Heavy loss, heavy grief, heavy all our fate!

In the same text, there are numerous other hiddenness passages that share this tone of anguish, regret, and perplexity.

Even within the pages of the Bible such laments are to be found. Psalm 22 begins with the plaintive cry,

My God, my God, why hast Thou forsaken me? . . . I cry by day, but Thou dost not answer. (Vv. 1-2, NASB)

And Psalm 88 adds,

But I, O LORD, have cried out to Thee for help,
And in the morning my prayer comes before Thee.

> O LORD, why dost Thou reject my soul?
> Why dost Thou hide Thy face from me?
>
> (Vv. 13-14, NASB)

From the biblical documents, through many of the great mystical writings of the Western tradition, up to the present day, the phenomenon of the hiddenness of God has been an unavoidable topic of some of the most sensitive and honest religious writing.

It seems commonly to be thought that the problem of evil is the single greatest intellectual problem for religious belief. How could a benevolent, loving, and all-powerful God allow his creation to contain so much pain and suffering? The problem of the hiddenness of God may be at least as great a problem, if not a greater problem, for theism. Of course, there are close ties between the two issues. The problem of the hiddenness of God can be viewed as a limited version of the problem of evil: What could possibly justify a good God's allowing us to be afflicted with so great an evil as the deprivation of any clear awareness of his presence, a deprivation bemoaned by both the psalmist and the saint? Our lack of a clear vision of deity could be seen as just one more widely suffered form of evil, one more reason to cite in launching an argument against the credibility of theism. On the other hand, and, I think, more insightfully, the problem of evil can be seen as a subcategory of the problem of the hiddenness of God. What is so religiously problematic about all the suffering in the world is that it hides from our view the existence of the benevolent, loving providence proclaimed by the Judeo-Christian tradition. As many philosophers have realized, the problem of evil alone can be taken to generate no more than an argument to the conclusion that if there is a personal creator and sustainer of the world, then he is evil, or at least, in the words of Woody Allen, "an underachiever." The general problem of the hiddenness of God can be taken much more directly to support an atheistic denial that there is any personal creator and sustainer of the world of any kind. It is clearly a problem.

It is not unusual to come across religious attempts to explain the hiddenness of God that appeal only to certain features or aspects of God's nature. Without making any effort to trace the historical pedigree of such attempts, I want to set out the main outlines of a few notable versions of this sort of strategy for solving our problem.

One version of this type of maneuver takes the form of an appeal to divine *incorporeality*, to the fact that, as traditionally conceived, God is not a material being. From this perspective, God's hiddenness consists in the fact that God does not fall within our perceptual purview, and this in turn is to be explained by reference to the fact that God is neither a bodily nor an embodied being, and thus not the sort of being accessible to sense perception. To express surprise or dismay over divine hiddenness, on this view, is to evince a basic misunderstanding concerning the kind of being God is.

A second version of this sort of strategy is closely akin to the first, but rather than appealing specifically to God's incorporeality, it consists in a set of simple claims about divine *transcendence*. Surely, it is said, God transcends the world. The existence of God is something over and above, distinct from, the existence of the world or anything in the world. God is Wholly Other, and thus his being is in no way contained in the world. The divine is of a different order or level of being, so it should not perplex us in the least that in the ordinary course of affairs, as we live out our lives on our level of reality in this world, God is typically hidden from us.

A third, related stratagem is interestingly different from these two and can even be seen to stand in some tension with them. It involves an appeal to the divine attribute of *omnipresence,* understood in a particular way. This solution to our problem begins by pointing out that for something to be an object of recognition, or perceptual discrimination, it must have a delimited presence, marked off spatially or temporally from some perceptual background. There can be no detection of presence without absence. There must be borders or boundaries to an entity's presence if it is to be discernible. There must be that-where-it-is-not as well as that-where-it-is if it is to be seen at all as present. Since God is omnipresent, pervasive of all reality, and infinite, there are no divine boundaries to make perceptual discrimination possible. What seems to be a total absence of the divine is only an illusion produced by the reality of his all-encompassing presence.

Admittedly, each of these claims is interesting, but as purported solutions to the problem of the hiddenness of God they all fall to a single, decisive objection. Regardless of whether and how God is incorporeal, transcendent, or omnipresent, he is traditionally conceived of as a supremely powerful causal agent, a personal initiator of actions with purposes, intentions, powers, and even a divine correlate of desires. Nothing else about his nature can explain why it is that he doesn't *act* more decisively and dramatically in the world to disambiguate the world. The unique mode of his existence cannot block this question if in fact God is a causal agent capable of extraordinary action. And this is so central a commitment of the Judeo-Christian tradition as to be nonnegotiable as a component of theism. So any such appeals to other aspects of God's nature cannot alone suffice to answer the question of why God is hidden. It is not so much a question concerning what God is as concerning why he acts, or refrains from acting, as he does.

In his *Dialogues concerning Natural Religion,* the eigh-

teenth-century Scottish philosopher David Hume has his literary character Cleanthes say,

> Suppose, therefore, that an articulate voice were heard in the
> clouds, much louder and more melodious than any which
> human art could ever reach; suppose that this voice were
> extended in the same instant over all nations and spoke to
> each nation in its own language and dialect; suppose that the
> words delivered not only contain a just sense and meaning,
> but convey some instruction altogether worthy of a benevo-
> lent being superior to mankind — could you possibly hesitate
> a moment concerning the cause of this voice, and must you
> not instantly ascribe to it some design or purpose?

Hume represents Cleanthes as imagining that a dramatic
enough event could convince us that its cause was a God. In
one of his essays in his book *Without Feathers,* Woody Allen
recounts the biblical story of Abraham and Isaac. At one point
in the story, Abraham reports to his wife Sarah that God has
commanded him to sacrifice their only child. Challenged by
Sarah to show how he knows he was in contact with *God,*
Abraham replies,

> I know it was the Lord. It was a deep resonant voice, well
> modulated, and nobody in the desert can get a rumble in it
> like that.

Some decades ago, a Yale philosopher, the late Norwood
Russell Hanson, wrote an article called "What I Don't Believe."
In it, he suggested that, in his opinion, it is unreasonable to
believe in the existence of God. Hanson thought that none of
the traditional arguments for the existence of God succeeded
as compelling proofs, and he believed that there is not enough
evidence of any kind to support theism. But he claimed not to

THE HIDDEN GOD   93

be stubborn about the issue. He said he was willing to change his mind if confronted with the right kind of evidence, and went on to specify exactly what kind of evidence would convince him:

> Suppose . . . that on next Tuesday morning, just after breakfast, all of us in this one world are knocked to our knees by a percussive and ear-shattering thunderclap. Snow swirls; leaves drop from trees; the earth heaves and buckles; buildings topple and towers tumble; the sky is ablaze with an eerie, silvery light. Just then, as all the people of this world look up, the heavens open — the clouds pull apart — revealing an unbelievably immense and radiant Zeus-like figure, towering above us like a hundred Everests. He frowns darkly as lightning plays across the features of his Michaelangeloid face. He then points down — *at me!* — and exclaims, for every man, woman and child to hear "I have had quite enough of your too-clever logic-chopping and word-watching in matters of theology. Be assured, N. R. Hanson, that I do most certainly exist."

Although he is clearly having fun in this passage, Hanson goes on to say,

> Please do not dismiss this example as a playful, irreverent Disney-oid contrivance. The conceptual point here is that *if* such a remarkable event were to transpire, *I* for one should certainly be convinced that God does exist.

And in commenting on such imaginable, dramatic theophanies, Anthony O'Hear states that

> It is surely a burning question why, if there is a God, there are not such events, and why the miracles believers do claim either are buried in a murky and problematic past, or are cures

which are not unequivocally miraculous exceptions to natural regularities.

This is the challenge concerning the hiddenness of God: Why does God not act in such a way as to disambiguate the world for all his rational creatures? If there really were a God, wouldn't he do so? Conversely, isn't the fact that there are no such sufficiently dramatic and decisive manifestations of deity enough by itself to show that there is no such God as theism proclaims? This is the problem.

Theists cannot reasonably deny that, in some sense, God is hidden. In fact, many theists have thought it important to proclaim from the outset the hiddenness of God. In the *Pensées,* we find Pascal explaining that

> What can be seen on earth indicates neither the total absence, nor the manifest presence of divinity, but the presence of a hidden God. Everything bears this stamp. (449)

He also comments,

> God being thus hidden, any religion that does not say that God is hidden is not true, and any religion which does not explain why does not instruct. (242)

It is not something for theists to sweep under the rug but is rather a proper and important subject for religious instruction. So says Pascal.

But there are numerous critics who deny that theists can embrace the issue with such equanimity as that manifested by Pascal. In fact, there are some who seem to think that a rational theistic account or explanation of the hiddenness of God is impossible in principle. Hanson was himself one of these people. He believed that we have a general principle for evaluating any existence claim: in the absence of sufficient, publicly available evidence for the claim, or any other evident manifestation of the truth of the claim, we ought to believe it to be false. If someone claims that there is a large snake in my office and I look around very carefully, seeing absolutely no signs of such an unwelcome intruder, I ought to reject the claim and judge it false. Likewise with the claim that there is a God, Hanson thought: in the absence of any clear sign that there is such a being, we ought to deny it. We ought to be atheists. So to claim that there is a God who is hidden and to try to explain this hiddenness is, from Hanson's point of view, to forget the thrust of this important principle.

But Hanson was simply wrong. Exactly what rationally justifies me in denying that there is a snake in my office? A mere lack of any sign of a snake? Before I look around, I'll presumably lack any sign of a snake. But before I look around I'm in no position to make a negative judgment based on the fact that I don't yet see a snake. *Once* I look around very carefully, and *still* see nothing, I then can deny the claim with good reason. When I have thoroughly searched the office, I am in what philosophically we can call "good epistemic position" (from the Greek word *episteme,* meaning "knowledge") to make a judgment on the claim. I am in such a position that, if the claim was true, I would most likely have evidence that it was true. If I have good reason to believe that I am in good epistemic position for judging an existence claim and *in that position* still lack any sufficient evidence or other manifestation of the truth of the existence claim, *then* I am rationally justified in denying the claim. If I am certain that my epistemic position is as good as it can be relative to the existence claim in question, I may then even be rationally compelled to deny the claim.

What does all this mean? Hanson overlooked all these important qualifications. Rationally claiming that there is a God who is hidden and trying to give a reasonable explanation of that hiddenness would be impossible only if we all were *certain* that we were in the best epistemic position possible for judging the claim that there is a God and in that position we lacked compelling proof, sufficient evidence, or any other manifestation of God's existence. But that's not the way it is. So it is possible to believe that there is a God who is hidden and to try to explain that.

What direction can a plausible theistic account of divine hiddenness possibly take? We have seen already that it cannot consist in claims about God's nature alone. It must involve suggestions about God's intentions, about divine policies for action (or for inaction) responsible for the degree of theological ambiguity our world exhibits. Of course, hiddenness is a relational matter, so any instructive account of God's hiddenness to creatures may very well have to say as much about us as it does about God. And, of course, even the divine-nature theories of God's hiddenness make implicit use of conceptions of human nature or of the human condition. For why should God's transcendence, incorporeality, or omnipresence be thought to hide him from us unless we are implicitly assumed to be such that we cannot perceive that sort of being? Perhaps it is our finitude or our dependence on the bodily that serves as the obstacle to our sensing the presence of the God Who Is. Maybe it is thus something about our nature that, given the nature of God, is to be blamed.

Or perhaps it is rather some *defect* in us, in principle remediable, that is to blame. Many theologians have suggested that human sinfulness has broken our communion with our holy Creator, distorting the vision we have of his world. Immersed in the flesh, we are oblivious to the spirit; since God is spirit, we know him not.

When we think about it carefully, it is clear that divine-nature theories linked with human-nature theories, or with

human-defectiveness theories, still fail to solve the problem of
the hiddenness of God. All such theories, joined together and
employed in tandem, will still fall short of what is needed. For
any such accounts, as typically developed, may explain why we
do not see the ordinary handiwork of God in creation and in
his normal providential governing of the world as manifesting
him, or why we don't experience his indwelling presence spiritually in any sort of regular or continuous way, but they do
not offer any explanation of why God does not do more extraordinary, dramatic miracles to demonstrate his existence and
governance. In fact, as Hanson and O'Hear have pointed out,
this is a large part of the problem.

We need an account of God's hiddenness that offers a
conception not just of what God is and what we are but,
centrally, of what he is *doing* or, to put it another way, of why
he is not doing any more than he is in fact doing. We need
some adumbration of divine goals, purposes, or intentions that
would make divine hiddenness intelligible.

I believe there is to be found in Pascal's notes a partial
outline of a promising direction for explaining this central
religious fact of God's hiddenness. In the *Pensées* he says that

> We can understand nothing of God's works unless we accept
> the principle that he wished to blind some and enlighten
> others. (232)

Now, it must be admitted that on first reading, this is truly a
hard saying. Why would a loving and just God blind some and
enlighten others? Isn't this *unfair?* Wouldn't divine justice prevent such a selective treatment of God's creatures?

Well, it is a fact that not everyone claims God to be hidden;
at least, not everyone sees him as equally hidden. Many people
believe there is a God and think they have good grounds in
their personal experience for so believing. Some claim to have

seen miracles. More claim to have discerned the quiet workings
of a subtle yet faithful providence in their lives. But of course
many people deny all such things. The world is thus divided
between those who claim to see and those who claim not to
see. Some people migrate between these groups. This fact about
us is consistent with Pascal's claim about differential divine
treatment. But what about God? Why would God blind some
and enlighten others? There are some hints in Pascal's notes
worth exploring on this matter.

In one place Pascal writes,

> God wishes to move the will rather than the mind. Perfect
> clarity would help the mind and harm the will.
>   Humble their pride. (234)

In human development, the paramount importance attaches
not just to what we know but to what we *become* and *do*. Perfect
clarity, the free gift of unambiguous knowledge in matters of
religion might for many people be *dangerous,* Pascal may be
suggesting here, and thus no gift at all. This at least seems to
me to be what he is getting at. Note the mention of pride.
Elsewhere, he states that

> If there were no obscurity man would not feel his corruption:
> if there were no light man could not hope for a cure. Thus
> it is not only right but useful for us that God should be partly
> concealed and partly revealed, since it is equally dangerous
> for man to know God without knowing his own wretchedness
> as to know his own wretchedness without knowing God.
> (446)

One of the best-known Pascalian themes is that of the greatness
and wretchedness of humanity. To know our wretchedness
without knowing our greatness produces despair. To know our

greatness without realizing our wretchedness inflames our pride. To know God clearly without at the same time having a proper self-knowledge would likewise promote pridefulness, Pascal believes, since we would be tempted to exult in our capacity for divinity to the exclusion of realizing our weaknesses. Knowledge, as the apostle Paul says, puffs up.

We all know people who puff up quite easily. And it is a fascinating study in human psychology to see how the slightest encounter with the rich and famous, or the least brush with the great or near great, can sometimes give a person an inflated feeling of self-importance. On occasion, the remotest relation will do. The neighbor of a person whose brother knows the guy who cleans a popular singer's pool feels himself tied to the glamorous world of the music business and doesn't mind at all talking about it. And I do not caricature here. I must admit that I myself have regaled many friends with a story about how Dean Smith, the great basketball coach at the University of North Carolina, once gave me and my wife tickets to sit with Carolina fans at a UNC–Notre Dame basketball game, and we ended up sitting just a few feet away from *Michael Jordan,* an ex-Tar Heel who has become one of the most famous basketball players in history. I do not hesitate to tell the story of this event at the slightest opportunity. These few facts seem to enhance my status with any sports-minded crowd, especially when the story is properly embellished. And, now that I've mentioned it, I suppose I should provide a bit more detail.

Carolina won that game in the final six seconds, 60-58. The next time the two teams met, Coach Smith came through again and put us in the Chapel Hill section of seats in the Notre Dame arena, the Joyce Athletic and Convocation Center — to the great chagrin of all my students. This game, the number-one-ranked Tar Heels lost, in the last minutes of the game, by the score of 60-58! Same score, different winner.

To thank Dean Smith for the tickets, and to send him condolences for the loss, I packaged up a bottle of Bailey's Irish Cream Whiskey with a note that said, in part, "Here's a little something Irish that will be easier to swallow than the final score." I wrapped it up, addressed it, and took it to a package service to mail, UPS. The man at the counter told me to "Declare the Contents." I said, "Bailey's Irish Cream." He frowned and explained, "I'm sorry, that can't be shipped across state lines. It's against the law." I replied, "Oh, no, that's too bad. It was a present for Dean Smith." "Did you say *Dean Smith, the* Dean Smith?" he asked as he glanced down at the address. I told him the whole story and then reached for the package. He held it, thought for a moment, and said, "We'll call it 'glassware.'" It was stamped and shipped. Now he has a story too.

A short while later, I received a handwritten thank-you note from the Coach. In the state of North Carolina, my home state, this is the greatest sort of worldly event imaginable. My wife, also a native Tar Heel, held the note in her hands, overcome with a new sense of my importance, and said with great excitement: "A handwritten note from *Dean Smith!*" She paused, then added, "Now I know why I married you." My parents' minister back home in Durham, a man I had known since college, heard of it all and told my mother and father, "I always knew Tom would amount to something." All this as a result of a couple of pleasant conversations and a handwritten note from Dean Smith (oh, I didn't mention the conversations, did I?). A brush with greatness, a close encounter with celebrity or money or power, and the ego inflates like a rubber raft.

Pascal wants us to try to imagine what would happen if any of us came to know God in a close encounter without being properly prepared. His suggestion is that we would quickly hit the zenith of pridefulness, as many people do who falsely take themselves to be in special, intimate communion with God.

It is Pascal's view that

> Man's true nature, his true good and true virtue, and true religion are things which cannot be known separately. (393)

Religious knowledge without moral qualifications would be dangerous. It may even be impossible. Pascal believes that there are moral, dispositional, attitudinal requirements for acquiring some of the most important forms of knowledge.

> Truth is so obscured nowadays and lies so well established that unless we love the truth we shall never recognize it. (739)

Loving the truth is thus presented as a necessary condition for knowing the truth. Armchair theology is no more possible than armchair science. In both endeavors, activity is required, however different the sort of activity might be in the different realms.

Long before Pascal, the tie between *practice* (or behavior) and *theory* (or knowledge) was recognized and emphasized by Christian writers. From the pages of the New Testament through the writings of the early church theologians, this connection was reiterated again and again. In an important essay, "On the Incarnation of the Word," the prominent writer and early church leader St. Athanasius once even went so far as to say that "without a pure mind and a modeling of the life after the saints, a man could not possibly comprehend the words of the saints."

But what exactly is the relevance of all this to the hiddenness of God? It is fairly simple but at the same time subtle. Something of God's existence and nature can be properly known by a person only if he is at the appropriate developmental stage. Were God to reveal himself to people improperly prepared to come to know and love him, such revelation would be more of a curse than a blessing. In order to allow us to develop to the point at which a knowledge of him would be the extraordinarily positive thing it can potentially be, God must govern his public manifestation in accordance with the needs of the least developed of his human creatures. Only within the heart of the properly formed individual can more be safely offered. And there, such people claim, it *is* offered.

The development seen as so important for catching even a glimpse of the religious vision is largely a moral-spiritual development in proper self-estimation, the sort of self-assessment and attitudinal demeanor commonly known as *humility,* the desirable contrary of pridefulness. The obscurity that surrounds ultimate issues in this world conduces to our realization that we lack complete self-sufficiency. It provides for the dawning of a proper personal humility. In particular, our ignorance of the answers to our most ultimate questions goads us, if we are rational, into seeking the truth with all our energies. Of course, there is always the alternative strategy of retreating into one's own resources and, with Bertrand Russell, building the soul's habitation on a foundation of unyielding despair. But Pascal joins the biblical authors in saying that those who seek will find.

The importance of the search or the quest is a perennial religious theme in many different religious traditions. It is also something emphasized in many passages by Pascal. Seeking, of course, is widely regarded as having value on many sorts of occasions, in many differing circumstances, but value of only a certain simple sort of instrumental nature. Seeking for something is typically valuable insofar as and only insofar as finding it is valuable. The purpose of seeking is just finding. But in the religious context, when it comes to the ultimate questions, the activity of seeking takes on a new type of value. It may be that the act of seeking reinforces, entrenches, and develops both humility and the love for truth. It is this connection with humility, a quality that arguably is at the core of all moral virtue, that sheds light on the religious importance of the necessity of seeking imposed on us by the religious ambiguity of the world, by the darkness we are in.

There is perhaps no greater human need than the need every individual has for a proper self-image, a proper self-assessment, and, connected to this, a proper valuation of others. The vast majority of human beings fall into one or another of three categories: (1) those with an inflated, overly prideful self-image, (2) those with a wrongly low self-image, and (3) those who experience a pendulum problem of swinging back and forth between unreasonable pridefulness and inappropriate self-abasement. Few people know and value themselves properly. And if we can't know accurately what is nearest to each of us — our very own self — how can we expect to know more remote mysteries of life? We cannot know God without standing in the right relationship to God. We cannot know our true selves without standing in the right relationships to those selves. And all these relations are inextricably bound together. Receptivity to ultimate truth requires humility, and humility of the proper sort. We should be confident as seekers, but never arrogant, never presumptuous.

The problem is, humility never comes easily. And this manifests itself richly in human relations. The novelist Peter DeVries captures a stubborn truth about human nature with the humor of his opening line for the novel *The Prick of Noon:*

> The trouble with treating people as equals is that the first thing you know they may be doing the same thing to you.

The recognition of truth this evokes in many of us is, we should admit, a bit embarrassing. We are not comfortable with humility, or with coming anywhere near to humility. Pascal thinks of God as interested in this fact. And if indeed there is a God who created us and loves us and wants to draw us into a proper relationship to himself, it makes a great deal of sense, as we shall see, that he should take an interest in this fact and act accordingly.

Pascal approaches the problem of the hiddenness of God not just as a convinced theist but also as a committed Christian, as displayed in a passage from the *Pensées* where he specifies that

> Knowing God without knowing our own wretchedness makes for pride.
> Knowing our own wretchedness without knowing God makes for despair.
> Knowing Jesus Christ strikes the balance because he shows us both God and our own wretchedness. (192)

Jesus the Christ shows us God through his own divinity and shows us our wretchedness in contrast with the standard he presents of human perfection. In a particularly vivid passage, Pascal says,

> When everything is moving at once, nothing appears to be moving, as on board ship. When everyone is moving towards depravity, no one seems to be moving, but if someone stops, he shows up the others who are rushing on, by acting as a fixed point. (699)

We see our wretchedness as well in witnessing the fate he suffered at human hands. And it is not at all irrelevant, but extraordinarily revealing, that this fate, involving as it did extreme self-sacrifice and humility on the part of the God-man, unveils the deepest truth both about divinity and about the nature of perfected humanity. This is the Christian claim, so succinctly put by Pascal.

Although much more needs to be said, this direction of thought seems to me to be a most promising beginning for reflection on the hiddenness of God. It is a number of deep and subtle truths tied up with all this that I think lies behind Pascal's intimations of God's purposes in refraining from manifesting himself in more astounding public spectacles. And it is thus more than obnoxious cleverness when Pascal finally writes this short dialogue:

> 'Why does God not show himself?' — 'Are you worthy?' — 'Yes.' — 'You are very presumptuous, and thus unworthy.' — 'No.' — 'Then you are just unworthy.' (*Additional Pensées*, 13)

In the most intimately personal and absolutely important ultimate questions about life and about the deepest nature of the reality in which we all live, the name of the game is not drawing conclusions from complex proofs. The name of the game is changing your life, a theme we'll be returning to.

In the Gospel of John we are told that at one point in the controversial career of Jesus, a rabbinical teacher and a member of the ruling class that opposed Jesus, a man named Nicodemus, went to visit him at night, to speak with him under cover of darkness, when any personal risk would be minimized. We are told that he approached Jesus and said,

> Rabbi, we know that You have come from God as a teacher; for no one can do these signs that You do unless God is with him. (John 3:2, NASB)

This in itself was an extraordinary statement to come from the

mouth of a Pharisee. Despite all the pressure he must have felt
from his fellows to dismiss or denounce the ministry of Jesus,
Nicodemus was a clear enough thinker to have weighed the
evidence available to him and drawn his own conclusions. He
reasoned that, on the basis of the evidence he had seen, Jesus
must have had God with him. And he went to the trouble to
visit Jesus and inform him of this conclusion. He had obviously
attended well to what he had seen, he had appreciated its
significance, and he offered a valid inference to a true conclusion, breaking through the nearly monolithic animosity toward
Jesus to be found among his peers.

So, what did Jesus do? Did he welcome Nicodemus with joy,
congratulating him on his independence of mind, his theological
astuteness, and his rigor in reasoning? Did he say, "Splendid
argument! True conclusion! Well thought out!"? No, he did no
such thing. The text goes on immediately to report that

> Jesus answered and said to him, "Truly, truly, I say to you, unless
> one is born again, he cannot see the kingdom of God." (V. 3)

For years I did not understand this response, this "answer."
It bothered me tremendously. Whenever I read the passage, or
heard it read, I winced. My ears burned with embarrassment.
And, by some odd coincidence, or for some good reason, I
often heard these verses read. It sounded to me as if either Jesus
was just being rude to this man, ignoring what he had said and
changing the subject altogether, or else Jesus was not very good
in conversation and just missed the point of his remark and of
his nocturnal visit. An inquisitive man goes out of his way to
pay a social call and broaches an important topic only to be
addressed about some other sort of matter altogether. I didn't
understand. And Nicodemus didn't either. At least, not at first.
It was Pascal who helped me to grasp what Jesus was doing.

There are two ways to respond to a remark. Every question, every argument, every conversational statement embodies assumptions, is made from a perspective, and implicitly lays down rules for a proper response, for an appropriate answer. If you accept the assumptions, endorse the perspective, and find the rules appropriate, you can play the game launched by the question or comment and answer or otherwise respond to it on its own terms. Or you can change the game being played. If you judge that something is awry and needing correction, you can respond in a way that seems surprising, in a way meant to help your interlocutor see the light. This is precisely what Jesus was doing.

The name of the game for Nicodemus, it seems, was satisfying intellectual curiosity. He had changed his mind. But Jesus wanted him to change his life. So Jesus didn't play the game according to Nicodemus's rules. He did not encourage his theologizing. He did not praise his intellectual acumen. He challenged him to be "born again" — an odd and extreme metaphor for a necessary and extreme change of heart. Nicodemus had evidence, and perhaps he wanted more. Perhaps he wanted proof. He may have wanted to experience an endorsement of his conclusions. What he got was a nudge in a very different direction.

Pascal understood our craving for direct experience, evidence, and proof. And he believed that, in the end, the evidence would be available to those capable of seeing it. The experience would come. But he did not believe that pure reason could ferret out evidence and churn out proofs that would satisfy all doubters and draw us nearer to God. He did not believe that overwhelming dramatic religious experiences and evidences would be available to just anyone and everyone, regardless of their epistemic position.

We typically want to occupy neutral ground until all the

evidence is in. Pascal wants to show us that there really is no truly neutral ground on this vital matter and that until we occupy the right ground, the evidence we want is not going to become available.

Many of us who value truth are inclined to value experience and human reason as our most trustworthy avenues to the truth. We want our beliefs to be reasonable, and so we naturally seek to believe only those claims about reality for which we have good reasons — typically, clear experience, good evidence, or cogent arguments. We like to see for ourselves and to think things through for ourselves when we have the right background, training, and competence to do so. And when we are not in a position to judge for ourselves what beliefs are reasonable to hold, we depend on the judgment of other people who are themselves rightly positioned to make the right observations and to reason things through for themselves as well as for us.

As a mathematician and experimental scientist, Pascal was a champion of human observation and reason, properly understood. He was confident that when we discipline ourselves and work very hard to make the right observations, when we devise careful experiments, and when we make cautious inferences about what we have seen, we can arrive at scientific truth about our world. By such activities we get ourselves into good epistemic position to know the deepest truths about the physical universe. Pascal believed that other activities, just as difficult and just as important, can help us get into good epistemic position to judge the deepest philosophical and religious issues as well. He accordingly devised a fascinating argument to launch us into the appropriate endeavors, an argument that has both delighted and irritated people for centuries, and it is to that argument that we now turn.

7

WAGERING A LIFE

L IFE is risk. Nothing we do that is of any importance carries with it a guarantee of success. Nothing we *can* do is absolutely sure to secure even our own personal safety or well-being from one hour to the next. Yet we are constantly faced with choices. Lots of decisions, no guarantees.

We all, in some way or another, adopt strategies for living, ways of approaching the world, ways of making choices that aim at the attainment of what we consider good. These strategies are all, to some extent or another, calculated gambles. We have no compelling proofs that our strategies will work. None of them is a sure thing. But we are used to the risk. We are accustomed to living without many true certainties, to the extent that we ordinarily forget that life is risk.

Is there a God? Does human existence have an objective, unshakable meaning? Do our interests, projects, or loves survive beyond the narrow bounds of this transitory world? Over the centuries, many intelligent, reflective people have answered Yes to these questions. And many have answered No. Some of the yea-sayers have claimed direct, powerful personal experiences as the basis for their answer. It is a rare nay-sayer to have made his own such claim. Negative answers are usually based on some form of reasoning from what the nay-sayer takes to be relevant evidence. There are arguments against the existence of God, arguments against objective meaning in life, arguments against life after death. And there are arguments to the contrary, arguments affirming the existence of God, affirming objective meaning in life, and affirming the existence of life after death.

Arguments are rarely as powerful as direct experiences, however, and rarely as satisfying. When I get home for lunch, seeing my wife is always preferable to merely inferring her presence in the house from small bits of evidence. Likewise, having some experience of God would beat having any number of theistic arguments available for consideration. But for people who seem to lack any experiences sufficient for the answering of ultimate questions, what is left except argument?

In his attempt to recommend a Christian worldview to his unbelieving contemporaries, Pascal hit upon a rare form of argument, an argument meant to help them move themselves into a better position to have the sort of experience of the reality of God that they lacked and to experience as well the truth of the Christian message about right relations with God. Throughout human history, almost all the arguments that have been devised for or against a religious worldview have attempted to show that some central religious belief is either true or false. These arguments have attempted to establish or at least to raise the probability of some claim about the nature of ultimate reality. Pascal's intriguing argument is not like that at all. His argument attempts to show that, in light of the ultimate questions, we ought to adopt a certain kind of strategy for living, with the aim in view of coming to know, and attaining the proper relation to, the highest Truth. We all employ life strategies, and we all gamble with those strategies. Pascal devised an argument to show us that we all ought to bet our lives on God. It is known, appropriately enough, as *Pascal's Wager*.

Pascal begins to lay out the famous wager argument with this striking passage:

> "Either God is or he is not." But to which view shall we be inclined? Reason cannot decide this question. Infinite chaos separates us. At the far end of this infinite distance, a coin is being spun which will come down heads or tails. How will you wager? Reason cannot make you choose either, reason cannot prove either wrong.

In this life, there is no absolute proof available to the skeptic that there is a God. Nor is there any way of proving that there is not. Reason by itself cannot decide the issue. We live in a world that seems to many people deeply ambiguous. It does not clearly speak of its ultimate nature. There are some indications that a religious view of the world is true. There are some indications that it is not. Pascal asks each of us a simple question about this ultimate issue: *How will you wager?* He hopes to help us place the right bet.

Imagine a race between two horses. Let's say that they've competed many times before. Call them "Gold" and "Silver." Gold has come in first in two out of every three races they've had. Silver has finished ahead only one third of the time. Today you are at the track, as you have been many times before. You want to bet on this race, and you have to decide which horse to back. Gold is twice as likely to win, but there are some other factors to consider. How much does it cost to bet on Gold? On Silver? And what's the payoff if you bet on Gold and Gold wins? Correspondingly, what do you get if you successfully back Silver? All these factors must be taken into consideration.

There seem to be, at first thought, two different kinds of goals a gambler could have in placing his bets. One goal would be to minimize his losses. Another would be to maximize his gains. If someone cared only about the former, he wouldn't go to the track at all. He would stay at home. And to the extent that the loss minimization goal is valued, he will try to shy away from risk whenever possible. A regular gambler accustomed to risk presumably seeks to maximize his gains, and not just today or in one particular bet but over the long run. Pascal seems to have been one of the first people to help us understand that a rational gambler seeking to maximize his gains over the long run will place his bets in accordance with a certain calculation, a calculation that can be represented by a simple formula for the determining of what we can call *Expected Value:*

(EV): (Probability × Payoff) - Cost = Expected Value

Expected Value is an abstract guide to maximal gain over the long run. The rational gambler places the bet that has associated with it the highest Expected Value. I call the Expected Value of a bet an "abstract guide" only to make clear that it does not represent what will be won, concretely speaking. What will be won is the amount specified as "payoff." The gambler who bets in accordance with the highest Expected Value may lose a few more bets than the gambler who bets always in accordance with the highest probability, but because of the greater payoffs he gets when he does win and the lesser costs he typically incurs, these short-term losses allow for a greater gain in the long run.

Now, as a matter of fact, Expected Value often follows along with probability, so that the horse with the greatest chance of winning will also be the horse that carries with it the greatest Expected Value. But these measures can diverge. To see how, let's fill in our example a bit more. For the sake of simplicity, we'll use some highly artificial numbers.

Suppose that the payoff associated with Gold is three hundred dollars. To place a bet on Gold costs sixty dollars. The less likely Silver pays nine hundred dollars, and to bet on this

horse costs only twenty dollars. This can all be represented by
a simple chart:

Horse	Probability	Payoff	Cost	Expected Value
Gold	⅔	$300	$60	$140
Silver	⅓	$900	$20	$280

Again, the Expected Value is not the amount of money to be
placed in your hand at the end of this race if you bet on a
certain horse and win. It is the way of quantifying the overall
value of each bet in this particular wagering situation, all things
considered. Figuring the Expected Values of our two horses on
the basis of our formula, we find that Gold, the horse more
likely to win, has in this case the lower overall Expected Value.
Silver, the bet with the lower probability, enjoys the higher
Expected Value. Thus, in this particular case, the rational gambler seeking to maximize his gains over the long run places his
wager on Silver. Again, the particulars of this example have
been contrived in such a way as to show how it is possible for
Expected Value and probability to diverge, although very often
they go hand in hand.

Now we are in a position to see how all this can be applied
to considerations of religious belief. Pascal believed that Christian theism is true and, furthermore, that a fair, unbiased in-
quirer could come to see that there is a substantial body of
evidence in favor of its truth to be found in the world. Yet
hardly any of us are altogether fair and unbiased when we
consider ultimate issues. And what we are affects how much
we can see. At one point Pascal says,

> The prophecies, even the miracles and proofs of our religion,
> are not of such a kind that they can be said to be absolutely

convincing, but they are at the same time such that it cannot be said to be unreasonable to believe in them. There is thus evidence and obscurity, to enlighten some and obfuscate others. But the evidence is such as to exceed, or at least equal, the evidence to the contrary, so that it cannot be reason that decides us against following it, and can therefore only be concupiscence and wickedness of heart. (835)

He ends this passage with some strong words. In many of his notes, he makes the point that reason does not always call the shots in human life. Our deepest desires can affect not just what we do but even how we see the world. We so often see what we want to see and fail to see what we want not to see. Christian theism is true, and the evidence is there. It is such as to exceed, or at least equal, the evidence to the contrary. If we are rightly disposed to see it, we'll be able to see this evidence for what it is — a sign of the truth.

But what is all this evidence of which Pascal speaks? We'll have to spend the next two chapters laying some of it out for inspection. The evidence was important to Pascal. He was no irrationalist. As an empirical scientist, he recognized the vital role solid evidence should play in the forming of our beliefs. As a shrewd psychologist and a person of deep religious vision, however, he also realized how important our desires, emotions, attitudes, and patterns of action are when it comes to forming beliefs on ultimate issues.

Let us, for the sake of argument at this point, at least provisionally grant Pascal his view that, with respect to the claims of Christian theism, the world in which we live is ambiguous to many observers. There seems to be evidence both ways. If such a person were asked how probable is it that the Christian God exists, he might reply, "I don't know — 50/50, 60/40, 40/60 — it's unclear." Such an answer would express an appropriate level of uncertainty concerning the issue. But either the Christian God exists or the Christian God does not exist. If we had to assign numerical probabilities to reflect our degree of confidence over the issue, amid the conflict of apparent evidence we might likely find ourselves saying, "God, roughly one chance out of two; no such God, roughly the same."

Pascal believed that each of us is either betting for God — betting that there is a God — or betting against God — betting that there is no God — by the way we are living right now. There is nothing equivalent to staying home from the track. Either we are living as if there is a God, praying, seeking to determine God's will, and trying to live in accordance with those determinations, or we are living as if there is no God, refraining from or ignoring all such religious activities. There is, according to Pascal, no middle ground. We already are making one bet or the other. Which is it? Which should it be? If we find that our answers to these two questions diverge, it is not too late to change our wager.

Well, which bet should we make? Pascal thinks that there is no absolutely overwhelming argument for or against the existence of God, and no body of cumulative evidence on one side of the issue or the other that will compel us to see where the truth lies. Reason cannot force us to choose either answer; reason cannot prove either wrong. Pascal believes, however, that viewing the situation as a wager, as a rational gamble, can help us here to decide our course.

In order to construct an argument to assist us in determining which wager we should make, we need first to ask whether something can be said about the factors other than probability that are operative in this sort of decision. In the example of the horse race, we asked about payoffs and costs. Are there costs and benefits to be considered here as well? Pascal certainly thought so.

Imagine that we've thought over the various basic options available on the issue of whether there is a God, and we feel that the liveliest possibilities are Christian theism and atheism. We'll explore how we might get to this conclusion in the next two chapters. For now, let's just suppose that we have arrived at the point where we are contemplating these two alternatives of Christianity and atheism. They are, as a matter of fact, the two alternative worldviews most discussed, and viewed as rivals, in our culture. Are there costs associated with taking up either of these views of ultimate reality? The nonreligious person will certainly insist right away that, understood in any traditional sense, there are costs associated with being a Christian. Didn't Christ himself use the metaphor of taking up our own crosses to follow him? And the apostle Paul speaks prominently of sharing the sufferings of Christ. At a minimum, taking up a Christian worldview involves endorsing a perspective on the human condition that is not universally shared, and this can occasion offense on the part of people who do not share it. Christianity claims to offer to human beings the supreme revelation of God, the best account of divine-human relations, and the deepest truth about the only path to eternal salvation, the ultimate fulfillment for any creature. From an outsider's point of view, this can all sound quite presumptuous and arrogant. And the resulting annoyance can generate ill will — indeed, ill treatment.

But it might seem that a version of the same sort of cost can be incurred by the atheist. To take up an attitude of self-sufficiency in the world, or to deem that ultimate reality is best viewed as bereft of any loving intelligence (either at the top or the bottom, depending on which metaphor you prefer), can itself seem rather presumptuous as well. Pascal asks,

> what advantage is it to us to hear someone say he has shaken off the yoke, that he does not believe that there is a God

watching over his actions, that he considers himself sole master of his behaviour, and that he proposes to account for it to no one but himself? Does he think that by so doing he has henceforth won our full confidence, and made us expect from him consolation, counsel and assistance in all life's needs? Do they think that they have given us great pleasure by telling us that they hold our soul to be no more than wind or smoke, and saying it moreover in tones of pride and satisfaction? (427)

A profession of atheism, or a life lived in an atheistic direction, can also exact untoward social consequences, unless the person who makes this wager is subtle and cagey enough. I know atheists who attend church because they enjoy the beauties of liturgy. It is possible to be an atheist and enjoy the benefits of religious community, too, at least to some extent. It is possible to be an atheist *in secret*. Sufficiently well-disguised atheism need not alienate anyone in the way in which the sentiments of Pascal's smug unbeliever are likely to.

For that matter, it is hard to specify many costs an atheist is sure to incur up front, so to speak, while making his wager. Recall that in assigning costs to a bet, we cannot assume we know which horse will win the race. The costs we are looking into are the price of admission into the bet, the investment up front. We thus can't say here that the cost of betting against God is hell, or eternal separation from God, or a life without ultimate fulfillment. We can say that it is a life without a certain sort of hope, a kind of hope the religious believer does have. The atheist also denies himself access to a certain sort of psychological resource for transcending the vicissitudes of life in this world, a source of equanimity the believer has. But perhaps the mature atheist can develop his own psychological resources for handling life's ups and downs, for getting his bearings amid life's troubles.

The costs of casting one's lot with the religious seem by contrast, at least initially, fairly easy to specify. The Christian is called to avoid the sort of subtlety and social shrewdness that will hide his allegiance from public scrutiny. He is not to hide his light under a basket. But holding one's light aloft when people prefer the dark can be very difficult. Loving your neighbor as yourself can be very demanding. Not all neighbors are so lovable. Doing unto others as we would have them do unto us is not always easy in a world where we are most often tempted rather by a "first strike" mentality to do unto them *before* they do unto us. "Forsake not the assembling of yourselves together," the New Testament says. There are acts of worship to be performed. There are lessons to be learned. It's not always easy to drag your half-dead carcass to church on Sunday morning. There are pleasures to be shunned on some occasions, or at least with some people. One can drink deep from the tankard of pleasant sensation, but the truly religious person typically avoids total immersion, at least of the sort that, from the believer's point of view, too often drowns the unbeliever. We may even be called upon to suffer for the sake of others. Deprivation, sacrifice, the aggravations of enforced godliness, the demands of constant goodness or at least efforts at goodness — these are a lot for any naturally self-inclined individual to take. Are there costs incurred by the person who bets on God? I think an honest answer is "Yes." However, I think a more complete answer begins with "Yes, *but . . .* ," as we will now see.

Let's assume some very small initial cost for wagering on atheism, and a more significant cost for betting on God. We now need to ask about the payoffs or benefits associated with each bet. First, atheism.

What does the atheist win if he bets that there is no God and it turns out that he's right? Well, presumably, one benefit he will *not* derive will be the experience of finding out he was right. If there is no God, there probably is no life, or existence of an individual's conscious experiencing self, after death either. But even if there could be survival of bodily death in a Godless universe, it is hard to see how there could be any sort of experience on either side of the grave that would prove the atheist to have been right. If he is right, he will never experience the satisfaction of finding out for certain that he was right.

Is there then nothing to be gained from the atheistic wager? This would be the wrong conclusion to draw. The atheist derives a certain freedom from his wager, a freedom to do whatever he sees fit to do. He can design his own lifestyle. He can tailor it to fit his desires and his perceptions of the world as he chooses. If he is right, his conduct will not flout or violate any objective desiderata for human life, just in virtue of its having been atheistic. Now, I don't mean to imply that every atheist will be an unrestrained hedonist, following no law but the demands of his own desires. An atheist can believe that there are objective moral principles that should be obeyed, but it is awfully hard to give a convincing account of exactly what such principles consist in, where they might come from, or exactly what their status could be in a thoroughly physical system such as our universe is thought to be from an atheistic point of view. Or, without recognizing any objectivity to morality, an atheist can just choose to live in accordance with generally accepted morals. Or he can invent his own. Or he can live day to day in whatever way he chooses, varying his conduct with his mood. It is hard to see that much in this world is closed to him. He is a person focused on this world, since he believes it to be the only world there is. And from that field he can presumably reap any harvest he cares to. In the end, if he is right, nothing he has done in this world will have been doomed to failure simply in virtue of being atheistic.

But assuming, as most atheists do, that in an atheistic world death is the end of any human's existence, there will at best be only a finite number of benefits, or moments of benefit, to be derived from the wager against God, and this is significant. For when we consider the benefits to be derived from the Christian wager *if* it turns out to be right, we find something very different. The promise of eternal life, everlasting blissful communion with God and with those other fellow creatures who love God, is at the heart of the Christian faith. If Christianity turns out to be true, then anyone who has sincerely lived in a Christian way, relating himself to God as the Christian faith instructs, will find that he has been issued into a qualitatively superior form of life, consonant with the deepest truths about ultimate reality, a form of life that will be enjoyed, literally, forever.

If the Christian wager proves to be right, will the Christian enjoy the experience of satisfaction to be derived from finding out decisively that he is right? Even such staunch critics as Norwood Russell Hanson seem to acknowledge that the answer is "Yes." A range of experiences can easily be imagined that would preclude any reasonable doubts about what the outcome is if the Christian God does exist. So the Christian can have the satisfaction of finding that he was right. Moreover, if he loses the bet over whether there is a God, he will not be forced to face his error. For if there is no God and no existence beyond the moment of death, he can never have an experience beyond death that will disappoint. And if we were right in what we said about the atheist's inability on either side of the grave to enjoy an experience of finding out decisively that he is right, the same points will apply to the religious wagerer's finding out that he himself has been wrong. The disappointment of a decisive disproof is not to be dreaded. For the religious wager, it cannot materialize.

Here we have an interesting asymmetry, an interesting difference, between the two wagers. In fact we may even have a symmetrical asymmetry. The Christian wagerer can experience the profound satisfaction of discovering for sure that he was right, and he cannot experience the terrible disappointment of finding out for certain that he was wrong. The atheist, on the contrary, cannot experience any satisfaction from a discovery that he was right, and, moreover, *can*, according to the claims of the alternative, Christian theology, experience the terrible regret of discovering that he was wrong — that he lived his life in ignorance and disregard of the deepest truths of reality. Christian theology speaks of judgment, and it speaks of worse. Whatever is meant, it is plausible to suppose that it includes at least this sort of realization. So, in an important sense, we can say that for atheism there is a final no-satisfaction guarantee, whereas for theism, there is a final no-dissatisfaction guarantee.

Setting aside this last point, we can draw up a chart to represent our betting situation:

Bet	Probability	Payoff	Cost	Expected Value
Christianity	c ½	infinite	finite	infinite
Atheism	c ½	finite	small	finite

Even if we are unable to quantify more precisely the various factors to be considered in this wager, we can see what the outcome will be. Atheism brings with it, at best, only a finite expectation, whereas Christian theism carries with it an infinite Expected Value. No disparity could possibly be greater. Therefore, says Pascal, a rational gambler will bet on God.

Pascal himself develops the argument a bit differently. In his notes there are some enigmatic passages and also twists and turns of mathematical reasoning that are a bit more finely tuned than what we have considered. However, I think that the best of what he had in mind is well represented by what we have considered.

But some questions still need to be asked. If we find the reasoning persuasive, exactly how are we supposed to make the wager Pascal urges on us? Pascal anticipated this question and discusses it in a dialogue with an imaginary partner. His representative unbeliever has found that in considering the question of God, theoretical reason — the concern with discovering proofs of truth claims and evidence of truth — reaches an impasse. Pascal's argument, by contrast, can be considered an exercise in practical reasoning concerning how we ought to act. The unbeliever in Pascal's dialogue agrees to the force of Pascal's argument. He acknowledges that despite the uncertainty of theoretical reason, practical reason shows that he ought to bet on God. But there is a problem. The following exchange ensues:

UNBELIEVER: "Yes, but my hands are tied and my lips are sealed; I am being forced to wager and I am not free; I am being held fast and I am so made that I cannot believe. What do you want me to do then?"

PASCAL: "That is true, but at least get it into your head that, if you are unable to believe, it is because of your passions, since reason impels you to believe and yet you cannot do so. Concentrate then not on convincing yourself by multiplying proofs of God's existence but by diminishing your passions. You want to find faith and you do not know the road. You want to be cured of unbelief and you ask for the remedy: learn from

those who were once bound like you and who
now wager all they have. These are people who
know the road you wish to follow, who have
been cured of the affliction of which you wish
to be cured: follow the way by which they began.
They behaved just as if they did believe, taking
holy water, having masses said, and so on." (418)

Pascal goes on to say that as these people find themselves
engaged in religious wagering behavior, they naturally move in
the direction of true belief. His recommendation is that anyone
who sees the reasonableness of the wager should begin to enter
into a new pattern of living and thinking, insofar as he or she
finds it possible. The unbeliever should begin to attempt to
conform his life to a pattern set by true believers. He should
begin to think on the idea of God, he should meditate upon
moving religious stories, he should attempt to pray (as far as
that is possible), he should associate with people who already
believe and hold religious values to be very important, and he
should expose himself to religious rituals of worship. The recommendation of the wager argument is not "It is in your best
interest to believe in God, so therefore go and believe." Belief
is not under our direct voluntary control. If someone offered
me ten thousand dollars on the spot to believe right now that
within the next hour, without leaving my office, I will see
thirty-seven prize Indiana hogs wearing straw hats and dancing
to harmonica music, even though I never in the past have had
such an extraordinary porcine vision, I would find myself immediately well disposed to the proposition (a reward of ten
thousand dollars is quite an offer), but I would not be able to
just manufacture belief, even in response to the most lucrative
inducements. If something seems to me to be the case, I believe
it. I can't believe it if it does not seem to me to be the case,

regardless of how strong an argument might be presented to me to the effect that it is to my great advantage so to believe. I can *say* I believe it. I can project mentally or visualize in accordance with it, but if it doesn't seem to me to *be* true, I can't actually believe it is true, regardless of what I'm offered for so believing. And I think Pascal was a sufficiently shrewd psychologist to realize all this. He did not intend his wager argument to issue in an immediate *belief* in God, as a direct result. He intended it only to issue in a certain form of behavior, which would erode obstacles to belief, obstacles to be found in our emotions, attitudes, passions, and habitual ways of thinking and acting. He believed that religious behavior and religious thought would, at least over the long run, open the way to religious insight, to a perspicacious perception of religious reality. It is a complete and, unfortunately, common distortion of the human condition to think that what we see is altogether independent of what we do and how we feel. We can distinguish intellect from emotion, or reasoning from feeling, as an exercise in conceptual abstraction, and these are indeed distinguishable facets of the overall human grappling with the world, but we can't always separate what we distinguish in this way.

Open your eyes and you can see the physical world. But some truths about the physical world cannot be grasped without years of skilled preparation. Any normal thinking person can handle simple straightforward ideas, but there are tremendous reaches of the intellectual realm inaccessible to us apart from arduous training, persistent attention, and a firmly disciplined patience. The discernment of spiritual truth may also require certain capacities that in most of us desperately need cultivating. Pascalian wagering is best viewed as a determined attempt to cultivate those capacities on the part of people who, because of the great values involved, are gambling their lives, hoping for success.

To illustrate what Pascal has in mind, consider the following simple chart:

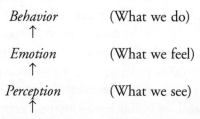

Behavior   (What we do)
↑

Emotion   (What we feel)
↑

Perception   (What we see)
↑

The Objective Situation (What we are in)

Ordinarily, we tend to think about life like this: the objective
situations we are in are responsible for what we perceive to be
true. What we perceive our circumstances to be in turn influ-
ences how we feel. It elicits one sort of attitude rather than
another, one set of emotions rather than another. And these
emotional and attitudinal states feed into our behavior. What
we do is affected by what we feel.

What Pascal wants us to see is that things can also work
the other way around. Action creates emotion. How we behave
can influence, over the long run and sometimes even on the
spot, what attitudes and emotions are operative in our lives.
And these in turn can open our eyes or blind us to aspects of
our objective environment. They can affect deeply our ability
to perceive the world aright. Emotions and attitudes can color
patterns of perception that either reveal to us or hide from us
the ultimate realities all around us. Reaching the objective
truth about any subtle and profound matter may require a
great deal of preparatory behavior, or wagering in the right
direction.

On the basis of his own experience, Pascal was convinced
that religious truth is present in the world to be perceived by
those who are capable of seeing. The evidence is out there to

be gathered, if we are prepared for it. But how much preparation should we undertake? Before launching into any new
enterprise, most of us would prefer to wait until all the evidence
is in. We want evidence up front that success, or fulfillment,
can be attained in this way. And often that means wanting
sufficient evidence for any of the distinctive assumptions upon
which the enterprise is predicated. I won't go into business
producing blankets unless I believe that there will continue to
be cold weather each year. But some enterprises require investment before all the evidence is in. Any successful entrepreneur
knows that. And in the realm of human relationships we discover this fairly early on. It is no oddity for this to be true of
religious involvement as well.

But some evidence is required up front. No one wants to
leap into utter darkness. The more investment an enterprise
requires, the more it costs to place the bet, the more evidence
we want before taking the first step. But of course, as Pascal
points out, it is not as if we can stay at home and keep all our
money in a safe bank until we get all the evidence we would
like. We are already moving down one road or the other. And
we can't even slow our movement. Are we now on the right
road? What is the evidence we have for betting against God,
evidence that an atheistic life is best hooked into the true
structure of reality? Considering all the benefits and costs relating to each of the rival bets, Pascal claims that the evidence
that can be marshaled for an atheistic worldview is inadequate.
He believes that the religious wager, by contrast, enjoys from
the start an adequate evidential base and, moreover, promises
to be able to extend that base.

So what is that evidence? Well, there is first of all a body
of evidence that *in this life* a person seeking to live in a genuinely
religious way is richly rewarded. Pascal even goes so far as to
say that

Only Christianity makes men both happy and lovable. (426)

Elsewhere he explains that

> The Christian's hope of possessing an infinite good is mingled
> with actual enjoyment as well as with fear, for, unlike people
> hoping for a kingdom of which they will have no part because
> they are subjects, Christians hope for holiness, and to be freed
> from unrighteousness, and some part of this is theirs already.
> (917)

Any individual engaged in Pascalian wagering must attempt to redirect his attention and energy from the natural
fixation we all have with our selves and considerations of self-
interest to a concern with God and with what he intends for
us, as reported in the Christian tradition. A Christian wagerer
initiates lines of conduct that lead to his gaining a new measure
of control over his passions, however imperfect that control
may yet be. A person making this wager with his or her life
will also have a transcendent focus and source of psychological
comfort in this world of turmoil and pain. The apostle Paul
described the results of the Christian life, fully lived, as the
production of a character full of love, joy, peace, patience,
kindness, goodness, faithfulness, gentleness, and self-control
(Gal. 5:22-23). To the extent that lives are changed as a result
of Christian living, to the extent that basic character disposi-
tions are transformed for the good during the process of wagering, evidence is produced that this wager is in accordance with
the deepest conditions for full and fulfilling human living.

But there is more, much more. And to some of that more,
we now need to turn.

8

THE HUMAN ENIGMA

W<small>E ARE</small> a puzzle to ourselves. The enigmas we face are not just hidden away high in the heavens or buried deep in the cosmic dust. One of the greatest mysteries is in us. How is the naked ape capable of grasping the mathematical structure of matter? How can one species produce both unspeakable wickedness and nearly inexplicable goodness? How can we be responsible both for the most disgusting squalor and for the most breathtaking beauty? How can grand aspirations and self-destructive impulses, kindness and cruelty, be interwoven in one life?

The human enigma cries out for explanation. Pascal believed that only the tenets of the Christian faith can adequately account for both the greatness and wretchedness of humanity. And he was convinced that this in itself is an important piece of evidence that Christianity embraces truth. No secular philosophical anthropology is as adequate as a Christian anthropology for diagnosing our ills and accounting for our strengths. Pascal saw the Christian account of human nature and the human condition as revelatory; he judged this to be a significant sign of its truth in all respects, and thus of its worthiness as an object of belief. There are many strands of evidence in favor of the truth of Christian theism, and in the next chapter we will look at a number of them that particularly impressed Pascal. But here we start from the heart of the matter. If a worldview cannot make sense of us, we cannot embrace it as giving us the sense of all else. So our look at the evidence must begin with what is most puzzling about us, about our lives, and must consider whether otherwise perplexing or inexplicable features of human existence might be powerfully explained by the claims of a traditional Christian theology. Of this, Pascal hoped to persuade us.

But, whatever its theoretical and evidentiary benefits, an inquiry into the human enigma has practical benefits for all. Pascal remarks,

> One must know oneself. Even if that does not help in finding truth, at least it helps in running one's life, and nothing is more proper. (72)

The proper study of humanity is humanity, Pope almost said; and Pascal might have added that the end of such study may be a glimpse of divinity.

There is a certain extraordinary futility to much of human behavior, a surprisingly repeated cycle of ungrounded hope and unexpected frustration driven by a seemingly insatiable desire. We are dissatisfied with our lives. We are dissatisfied with ourselves. And we desire change. In fact, we desire things whose acquisition we believe will bring that change. "If I could just live in a certain sort of house," "if I could just drive a particular kind of car," "if I could dress a certain way," "if I could gain a certain sort of reputation," we imagine, "my life would be different." The more we dream such dreams, the more we become dissatisfied with what we have and with what we are. The more dissatisfied we become, the more desirous we grow for change. Our hope is attached to some one thing, or collection of things, that would make all the difference. And it never does. Thus, the cycle repeats.

Typically, the quest is for what we think will give us pleasure, in such a way and to such an extent that our lives will be elevated to a new level, a level at which we can be satisfied and, finally, happy. Pascal comments,

> What causes inconstancy is the realization that present pleasures are false, together with the failure to realize that absent pleasures are vain. (73)

Present pleasures are false. They have failed to fulfill their promise to satisfy completely. And absent pleasures are vain. Those pleasures that we have not yet experienced call to us with their insistent and nearly irresistible siren song. But, Pascal assures us, their promises are just as empty. There is no earthly enjoyment that will bring a life to completeness. Life in this world can be a roller coaster ride from peaks of excitement to valleys of ennui. Or it can be like a trek through a desert of boredom relieved only by an occasional mirage. One of Pascal's shorter notes says:

> *Man's condition.* Inconstancy, boredom, anxiety. (24)

We hope, we fear, we despair.

But this sounds like an exceedingly bleak portrayal of human life. We aren't all anxious, bored, or desperate for change. No, but to the extent that we are living our lives only within the confines of what this world has to offer, Pascal thinks, we escape these problems only by weaving about ourselves a cocoon of illusion. There is a difference between being happy and merely imagining that we are happy.

Long ago Plato drew our attention to the importance of the distinction between appearance and reality. To those of us who do not have it, wealth and fame can appear to promise satisfaction and happiness. We can live within the appearance of the promise as we seek to acquire and even as we succeed in acquiring such things. But those who have seen through the illusion — Tolstoy and Pascal, for example — assure us that this is just appearance and not reality. Yet how easy it is to be caught up in a world of appearance! One way we weave an illusion about ourselves is by continuing to create an image of ourselves in the minds of other people, an image of talent, character, success, and satisfaction. And if we succeed in this, it may be our only real success and our only source of satisfaction. But surely this sort of successful illusion is nothing more than an illusion of success. We cannot attain true happiness by allowing ourselves to be caught up in the imaginary self we have created for the sake of others. And yet such an illusion can sustain us for a surprisingly long time, a time during which we are diverted from confronting the realities of our state. On this problem Pascal says,

> We are not satisfied with the life we have in ourselves and our own being. We want to lead an imaginary life in the eyes of others, and so we try to make an impression. We strive constantly to embellish and preserve our imaginary being, and neglect the real one. And if we are calm, or generous, or loyal, we are anxious to have it known so that we can attach these virtues to our other existence; we prefer to detach them from our real self so as to unite them with the other. We would cheerfully be cowards if that would acquire us a reputation for bravery. How clear a sign of the nullity of our own being that we are not satisfied with one without the other and often exchange one for the other! (806)

When, lacking true happiness, we are imagining ourselves to be happy, we need the support of the imaginations of others. The less we are really happy, the more we need the appearance of happiness to feed any illusion we have to the contrary. Consequently, the busier we are in creating an image, the clearer a sign we have that all is not right in our lives.

What does it take to really attain happiness? What does it take to attain real happiness? A longer passage from the *Pensées* will be illuminating here.

> All men seek happiness. There are no exceptions. However different the means they may employ, they all strive towards this goal! The reason why some go to war and some do not is the same desire in both, but interpreted in two different ways. The will never takes the least step except to that end. This is the motive of every act of every man, including those who go and hang themselves.
>
> Yet for very many years no one without faith has ever reached the goal at which everyone is continually aiming. All men complain: princes, subjects, nobles, commoners, old, young, strong, weak, learned, ignorant, healthy, sick, in every country, at every time, of all ages, and all conditions.
>
> A test which has gone on so long, without pause or change, really ought to convince us that we are incapable of attaining the good by our own efforts. But example teaches us very little. No two examples are so exactly alike that there is not some subtle difference, and that is what makes us expect that our expectations will not be disappointed this time as they were last time. So, while the present never satisfies us, experience deceives us, and leads us from one misfortune to another until death comes as the ultimate and eternal climax. (148)

As a bumper sticker I recently saw on a pickup truck so succinctly put it,

LIFE IS A BITCH, AND THEN YOU DIE.

But, back to Pascal. He continues:

> What else does this craving, and this helplessness, pro-
> claim but that there was once in man a true happiness, of
> which all that now remains is the empty print and trace? This
> he tries in vain to fill with everything around him, seeking in
> things that are not there the help he cannot find in those that
> are, though none can help, since this infinite abyss can be
> filled only with an infinite and immutable object; in other
> words, by God himself.
> God alone is man's true good. (148)

All the genuine unhappiness in this world is a sign that true
happiness is not to be found within its confines. Our incon-
stancy can be cured by only one constant. Our infinite desire
can be satisfied only by an infinite being. Our plight is evidence
of the truth about our place. Our place, in the great scheme
of things, is to be with God, in communion with and obedience
to our Creator, for whom we were created.

Out of place, we are wretched. But our wretchedness, Pascal
claims, is that of a dispossessed king. The nature of our
wretchedness reverberates with echoes of our greatness. And
this is true of so many facets of human wretchedness. Consider
for a moment the extraordinarily creative cruelty of which
human beings are capable. We are not like the animals who
fight and kill only for food or for the other necessities of
survival, such as territory, shelter, and reproduction. As any
homicide detective can attest, human beings are capable of
utterly gratuitous and demonically creative acts of terror and
torture. And in less dramatic fashion, human relations can call
forth emotional cruelty of astonishing dimensions and almost
artistic intricacy. From a Pascalian perspective, these are all dark
shadows of our having been created in the image of God *(imago*

Dei), with all the potential for creativity and freedom that entails. The wretchedness of our history reflects in a direct and perverse way the greatness of our original nature.

In the pages of the *Pensées*, Pascal seeks to characterize many aspects and manifestations of human wretchedness. The ancient Greek philosopher Protagoras once proclaimed that "man is the measure of all things." Pascal points out how in so many ways we are radically out of sync with the true measure of things. We exist suspended between two infinities, Pascal says, the realm of the incredibly small and the sweep of the immeasurably great. Meditation on our disproportionality can be extremely disturbing. We are out of sync with the natural world. And we are out of sync with each other. What is justice? What constitutes a good and just social order? Societies disagree. And often reflecting those disagreements, while introducing many more, philosophers disagree. What are the ultimate truths about reality? What is the reach of reason? We are awash in a sea of ideas with no sure anchorage. We are out of sync with Truth. Pascal represents well the perplexity of many of us when he says,

> When I consider the brief span of my life absorbed into the eternity which comes before and after — *as the remembrance of a guest that tarrieth but a day* — the small space I occupy and which I see swallowed up in the infinite immensity of spaces of which I know nothing and which know nothing of me, I take fright and am amazed to see myself here rather than there: there is no reason for me to be here rather than there, now rather than then. Who put me here? by whose command and act were this time and place allotted to me? (68)

We are disoriented. We are out of sync with time:

We never keep to the present. We recall the past; we anticipate
the future as if we found it too slow in coming and were
trying to hurry it up, or we recall the past as if to stay its too
rapid flight. We are so unwise that we wander about in times
that do not belong to us, and do not think of the only one
that does; so vain that we dream of times that are not and
blindly flee the only one that is. The fact is that the present
usually hurts. . . . The present is never our end. The past and
the present are our means, the future alone our end. Thus we
never actually live, but hope to live, and since we are always
planning how to be happy, it is inevitable that we should
never be so. (47)

Our existence is disjointed. We are disoriented. We do not
mesh with reality. This is not the portrait of a being who is the
measure of all things.

Human wretchedness is manifest in myriad ways. But it
consists most fundamentally in what Pascal calls "blindness and
concupiscence."

That is the state in which men are today. They retain some
feeble instinct from the happiness of their first nature, and
are plunged into the wretchedness of their blindness and
concupiscence, which has become their second nature. (149)

Pascal believes that outside the transforming power of Christian
faith, we are all trapped in habitual patterns of badly misplaced
thought and desire. Our habitual patterns of thought render
us blind to the deepest truths about reality and about ourselves.
And our habitual pattern of desire — desire out of control —
is what he refers to as "concupiscence," and he sees it as a
consuming fire.

It is one thing to identify most fundamentally what human
wretchedness is. It is quite another to explain how it arises. And

to provide such an explanation, Pascal believes, we must embrace apparent paradox. Of course, there is a sense in which
we are already well within the realm of the paradoxical whenever we are dealing with the human enigma. At one point, after
juxtaposing the human need for truth with the weakness of the
tools we use to launch our quest for it, Pascal exclaims,

> What sort of freak then is man! How novel, how monstrous,
> how chaotic, how paradoxical, how prodigious! Judge of all
> things, feeble earthworm, repository of truth, sink of doubt
> and error, glory and refuse of the universe!

He goes on to thunder,

> Know then, proud man, what a paradox you are to your-
> self. Be humble, impotent reason! Be silent, feeble nature!
> Learn that man infinitely transcends man, hear from your
> master your true condition, which is unknown to you.
> Listen to God. (131)

The human condition itself is paradoxical as it weaves wretchedness and greatness together. The passage from Pascal continues:

> Is it not as clear as day that man's condition is dual? The
> point is that if man had never been corrupted, he would, in
> his innocence, confidently enjoy both truth and felicity, and,
> if man had never been anything but corrupt, he would have
> no idea either of truth or bliss. But unhappy as we are (and
> we should be less so if there were no element of greatness in
> our condition) we have an idea of happiness but we cannot
> attain it. We perceive an image of the truth and possess
> nothing but falsehood, being equally incapable of absolute
> ignorance and certain knowledge; so obvious is it that we
> once enjoyed a degree of perfection from which we have
> unhappily fallen. (131)

Pascal here hints at the central Christian doctrines of creation and original sin: we were created by God, in the image of God, to enjoy blissful fellowship with God and God's creatures. But from this height we have fallen, and the extent of the fall is reflected in the enormity of our plight.

The doctrines of creation and the fall, or of creation and original sin, allow us to recognize and understand the full extent of the human paradox, the extremes of greatness and wretchedness bound together.

> (After hearing the whole nature of man.) For a religion to be true it must have known our nature; it must have known its greatness and smallness, and the reason for both. What other religion but Christianity has known this? (215)

It was Pascal's view that human philosophers operating independently of divine revelation inevitably have gotten it wrong, either becoming blind to human wretchedness because of their focus on human greatness, or losing sight of our greatness because of a fixation on our wretchedness. The one mistake produces pridefulness, the other despair. Only by keeping both truths in view from the perspective of Christian theology can we attain the proper attitude of hope tinged with humility. An understanding of our greatness grounds our hope, and, conjoined with a proper assessment of our wretchedness, it gives rise to humility, perhaps the chief of human virtues from a Christian point of view.

Why does any of us have hope? Because of the traces of greatness within. Why does any of us despair? Because we compare what we perceive to be our present state and likely prospects with the aspirations we have deep down that are connected to those traces of greatness within. And why do we all go wrong? Why are there habitual patterns of badly misplaced thought and desire within the life of every one of us? Is it just an overwhelmingly astonishing coincidence? Or is there some explanation? Pascal suggests that Christian theology offers an explanation that involves, in part, another apparent paradox — the doctrine of original sin. Why do we all go wrong? It is not just a coincidence; it is because of original sin.

Pascal reads the Bible in a very traditional, old-fashioned way. He takes its statements at face value unless he believes he has good reason not to do so. Consequently, he reads the Old and New Testaments as claiming that there was in human history an original falling away from our intended relationship to God and that our present plight results in part from that. This, in the most general terms possible, is the doctrine of original sin.

Until the modern era, most readers of the Bible have taken the doctrine to be something like this: God created a first man, Adam, and a first woman, Eve, to live in loving communion with him and to rule over the earth, with their offspring, in obedience to his commands. These first human beings disobeyed God and fell from communion with him. In so doing they became guilty of sin, and their guilt was subsequently passed along to their offspring, ultimately to all created human beings, who can be rescued from that objective guilt, along with its consequences, only by the saving work of Christ, the Son of God, who came to earth for the purpose of freeing us from the results of that original sin and thus to make it possible for us once again to enter into the intended relationship to God for which we were created.

This traditional understanding of the doctrine of original sin involves assumptions about how the Bible is to be interpreted, beliefs about the history of human life on earth, and categories of moral thought that are strikingly out of fashion among most academically trained theologians nowadays. The story of Adam and Eve has been labeled a "myth" and is thought to be, at best, symbolic of the condition of every normal human being in his or her development from moral innocence to self-conscious moral autonomy. The idea of guilt being passed along from generation to generation is judged to be completely beyond the pale, and it is rejected along with the historical dimension of the doctrine. Every man may have an original sin in his life, every woman in hers, and this may affect subsequent actions within the same life, but any notion of interpersonal transmission of sin, or its effects, is left aside.

Pascal recognized the paradoxical nature of the traditional doctrine, the idea that we could now be guilty as a result of some act we ourselves did not perform but that was performed by someone else long ago. Guilt is tied to responsibility, and that to ownership. I can be objectively guilty only for my own wrongdoing, for which I and I alone am morally responsible. Guilt resulting from an act that is not mine is, Pascal realized, a paradoxical idea at best:

> Without doubt nothing is more shocking to our reason than to say that the sin of the first man has implicated in its guilt men so far from the original sin that they seem incapable of sharing it. This flow of guilt does not seem merely impossible to us, but indeed most unjust. What could be more contrary to the rules of our miserable justice than the eternal damnation of a child, incapable of will, for an act in which he seems to have so little part that it was actually committed 6,000 years before he existed? Certainly nothing jolts us more rudely than this doctrine, and yet, but for this mystery, the most incomprehensible of all, we remain incomprehensible to ourselves. The knot of our condition was twisted and turned in that abyss, so that it is harder to conceive of man without this mystery than for man to conceive of it himself. (131)

Pascal embraced the most difficult version of the doctrine, the version that seems most counterintuitive and morally unacceptable, and he maintained that it alone could account for our wretched condition. On this point I believe Pascal may have gotten a little carried away in his employment of what is, in other respects, a fascinating and insightful argumentative strategy.

Pascal wants to persuade us of the truth of the Christian religion. So, as we shall see in the next chapter, he marshals all kinds of evidence for its truth. Sometimes he appears to exult in focusing on something that seems to be a problem for Christian theology, a weakness in the case for Christian truth, and, through a clever reversal, turning it into a strength. This is an interesting strategy. He is convinced that Christian theology of a very traditional sort is true, so he is confident to take up those awkward or perplexing issues that most religious people would prefer to avoid. Indeed, he even seems to fix upon them as particularly striking issues for displaying the truth of the faith.

The idea seems to be something like this: whatever claims or aspects of Christian theology are nearest to the general deliverances of sound common sense will not serve as dramatic marks of Christianity's divine origin. Any sufficiently reflective person could have thought them up. But whatever in Christian doctrine is hardest to understand, by contrast, must ultimately provide the deepest truth, and thus the truth most likely to be recognized as divine in origin.

There is clearly something very insightful and sensible about such an argumentative strategy. The danger, however, is that it can incline a practitioner to relish unduly paradoxical, difficult, or mysterious interpretations of doctrines to the neglect of more sensible or intelligible versions, themselves helpfully insightful. In dealing with the doctrine of original sin, I think Pascal was a little too enthralled with this strategy. If an idea is far enough away from anything remotely recognizable as true by reflective common sense, it just cannot serve as a sign or mark of the true religion for the purposes of those seeking truth. It will not lead any sensible person to embrace Christian faith unless it can somehow be made itself to look true. Once one *is* a Christian, one can learn to live with difficulties we cannot fully understand. Who are we, after all, to expect to understand *everything*? But up front, so to speak, in trying to present evidence that Christianity is true, Pascal could have drawn our attention to features of the doctrine of original sin that together can add up to an alternative interpretation of it and that do make a great deal of sense of the human condition despite containing some slight remnant of paradox.

The traditional version of the doctrine of original sin embraced by Pascal we can refer to as "the Transmission of Guilt version." Another version of the doctrine is available that we can refer to as "the Transmission of Damage version." This version will be sufficient for explaining what needs to be explained here about the human condition without requiring us to believe, or see as insightful, something that seems impossible and unjust.

At some point in time, sin entered the world. Whether we believe in a single first sin or not, we can acknowledge this. Even if the history of moral evil on this earth was inaugurated with thirty-seven simultaneous wrongdoings, the time of their occurrence was a point at which, through thirty-seven portals, sin entered the world. And once wrongdoing enters the world, the world is never the same again. Sin inevitably changes the dynamic of interpersonal relations, which in turn inevitably affects the actions of other individuals. Our ancestors and our contemporaries have gone wrong. They have acted immorally. And they have thereby created or reinforced conditions that encourage our going wrong as well. And we do. We all go wrong; we all sin and thereby create or reinforce conditions that encourage others to go wrong as well. No man is an island. It is not the case that an individual's free acts flow out of his free choices alone. Who is doing the choosing? Who he is and how he chooses results, at least in part, from the nature of the society in which he has developed, which, in turn, results from who the other individuals in his society are and how they choose.

Traditional theologians and Christian preachers have long proclaimed that "we are all born in sin." This is true, but perhaps a bit misleading. We all come to be *as persons* in a sinful society. Sin has entered the world, and the damage has been transmitted to all subsequent generations. No act is an isolated event. Every act affects the actor, and every actor contributes by what he is and what he does to the society shared by his fellows, the society in which subsequent generations are raised.

Long ago, Christian theology explains, human beings broke free of a proper relation to their Creator. This resulted in disharmony within, disharmony among fellow humans, and disharmony with nature. The consequences of this fall have been transmitted ever since, throughout the human community. It is thus no surprise that we all go wrong. It is no extraordinary coincidence that we all display some degree of wretchedness. We all are formed in conditions traceable to that point of original sin. Any worldview that denies our insularity and proclaims our solidarity captures some facet of the truth. Any worldview that can explain our wretchedness without denying our greatness goes further. Any view that can give an equally insightful account of both does all that can be expected in this particular domain of philosophical anthropology.

It is Pascal's assertion that Christian theism does it all, and in just the right way. As created in the image of God, we are capable of knowing God. As fallen and sinful, we are not worthy of knowing God. But we are capable of being made worthy. And in these capacities our greatness is to be seen.

A proper self-esteem, a proper sense of self-worth and dignity, is one of the most elusive quarries for most of us in this life. Some of us are puffed up with pride. Others wallow in despair. Many of us vacillate between the two, sometimes entertaining too inflated a sense of self-worth, at other times tremendously depreciating our value. As creatures of God, Pascal believes, we are of equal and infinite value. As sinners who cut ourselves off from God, we are equally undeserving of his grace. But as objects of his never-ending love, as manifested in Christ, we are equally offered that grace. Unfortunately, we respond unequally.

In the story of Jesus the Christ we see the greatness of God's love, the greatness of our worth, the wretchedness of our state, and the prospects for our transformation. In the New Testament portrait of Jesus we see a sense of self suffused with humility and inspired with greatness. We have in his person, Pascal thinks, the great clue to unraveling the enigma that is ourselves and to discovering the mystery that is God. What we know about ourselves moves us to consider seriously the claims of the Christian faith. And what we cannot know about ourselves without the revelations of the Christian faith stands as a testimony to its truth. Pascal believed that the diagnosis of the human condition offered by Christianity was one of the marks of its truth available for our inspection. He also believed that there are many more marks of its truth, to some of which we should now turn.

9

MARKS OF THE TRUTH

Toward the beginning of the *Pensées,* Pascal wrote this note to himself:

> *Order.* Men despise religion. They hate it and are afraid it may be true. The cure for this is first to show that religion is not contrary to reason, but worthy of reverence and respect.
>
> Next make it attractive, make good men wish it were true, and then show that it is.
>
> Worthy of reverence because it really understands human nature.
>
> Attractive because it promises true good. (12)

Pascal was aware that, very often, we see only what we want to see. He believed that if he could convince us of our wretchedness and ultimate hopelessness without God and of the tremendous attractiveness of the most sophisticated and subtle insights and promises offered by Christian claims, then he might be able to overcome the natural reluctance many of us feel concerning some features of a religious worldview and open our eyes to see the evidence that is available for Christian truth.

Men despise religion. They hate it and are afraid it may be

true. There may seem to be many sources for this abhorrence, but they can be traced to a single root. Truly religious people must humble themselves in the worship and obedience of a creator they do not see. From a nonreligious point of view this can seem objectionable in a number of ways. First, there is the religious person's belief in the unseen. There is no public perceptual contact with the divine. Nor is there any range of public perceptual contact with the world that can be used to generate an incontrovertible proof of the reality of the divine. It is easy for the outsider then to assume that religious belief is contrary to reason.

Second, to believe in a personal creator in whose image we are made, a creator whose nature and actions define goodness, is to believe that we are not sole masters of our own destinies. There is a normative ground of our existence. We are answerable to a final authority not of our own making. To acknowledge such a cosmic order is to give up one's perceived autonomy, at least in principle. For the unbeliever who values his or her independence as a free being in the world, this can appear as an ultimate act of existential cowardice, a refusal to take one's life into one's own hands, a shirking of ultimate responsibility, a refusal to say "the buck stops here." Everything is referred to God. Every believer defers to the Creator. Politically, we stand in a stream of centuries of human struggle against sovereignty, tyranny, nondemocratically centralized and perpetuated authority. A religious worldview can just seem to embrace at the deepest level what we have been struggling to escape in our social arrangements. It can thus seem to be a retrograde and subversive force inimical to the whole direction of modern enlightened human development. Moreover, to put such high-sounding objections aside, to give up one's perceived autonomy is to give up one's sense that anything goes, that we can make, and break, our own rules, with only ourselves to answer to. To

believe in a perfectly good Creator whose nature and actions
provide a standard for our own character and acts can seem
very restrictive to an outsider.

Third, the whole attitudinal demeanor of worship and
obedience can seem contrary to human dignity. Some would
say that to believe in a being as exalted as a perfect God
diminishes one's own relative worth to a vanishing point. It
involves seeing humility as a fundamentally appropriate human
attitude. And perhaps nothing could be further from the direction of our natural attitudinal tendencies than a basic, nonnegotiable, perpetual sense of humility.

It is for reasons such as these that people can come to
despise religion. But on close inspection, it can be seen that
they are all bad reasons. It was Pascal's view that religion need
not be at all contrary to reason but rather in deep harmony
with it. And the sort of political freedom that people have
fought for throughout most of human history should not be
thought of as at all inconsistent with the ultimate authority of
a Creator over all. On the contrary, many people have argued
that the case for democracy can be made most strongly from
the perspective of a worldview in accordance with which all
human beings are created with equal, eternal, and infinite value
in the image of God. Outside such a worldview the case for
political equality is more difficult to establish. And finally, the
sort of personal humility called for by Christian faith is the
wellspring for all of those characteristics that can be thought
of as Christian virtues. Such humility is indeed contrary to the
demands of concupiscence. But Pascal thinks that the life of
unbridled, self-aggrandizing desire is not at all attractive or
satisfying. He believes that the Christian faith offers us all a
more attractive and fulfilling approach to life. If he can open
us up to this possibility, it is possible that he can open us up
to the evidence that exists for the truth of Christian claims. In

this chapter we need to survey, however briefly, some of the many strands of evidence he thinks there are. Pascal is convinced that God has not left himself without a witness. There are many marks of the truth available for our inspection, if we can just open ourselves to considering them fairly.

One important sign of the truth of the Christian religion, Pascal believed, is its account of human nature and its diagnosis of the human condition, as we noted in the previous chapter. Every religion involves a threefold conceptual structure: (1) a diagnosis of what is awry in human life, (2) a conception of ideal human existence, and (3) the specification of a path of salvation, a route from our current plight to that ideal state. For a religion to seem true, to seem to be in touch with reality, it must offer us plausible or sensible claims on these three matters. Pascal seemed to think that a Christian anthropology could be drawn from the resources of the Bible that would take care of the tasks of diagnosis and idealization with great plausibility. To the extent that Christian accounts of human wretchedness and greatness make sense, to the extent that they strike a chord of plausibility in us — to that extent a Christian anthropology can serve as a mark of the truth of Christian theology as a whole.

But how plausible is the specification of a path of salvation, the central procedure for attaining (or regaining) human wholeness, to be found in Christian theology? Of course, Christianity is built around the claim that the God who created the universe has acted uniquely in the birth, life, death, and resurrection of Jesus of Nazareth to effect salvation for all human beings who rightly relate themselves to God through him, in faith and obedience. In asking about the plausibility of the Christian faith as a whole, then, it is natural to ask about the claims it makes concerning this route to human wholeness.

Pascal hints at an argument that is relevant here. We can call it *the success argument*. He first points out that Christ demands that we give up our own efforts to get the most out of life and trust him instead to confer on us benefits the world cannot produce. But can we manage to break our servitude to our desires for the things of this world? Is it even possible that we so reorient our lives? It has happened, Pascal points out, through the preaching of the Christian gospel. Wherever Christ has been preached, lives have been changed, and changed dramatically. A good deal earlier than the time of Christ, the great philosopher Plato urged that we turn our attention away from our typical preoccupation with the mundane enticements of this world and focus on another, higher realm. But to what effect, by comparison, did this greatest of the philosophers work?

> What Plato had not been able to make a few chosen and highly educated men believe, a secret force made hundreds of thousands of ignorant men believe by the power of a few words. (338)

The contrast is quite stark and can seem to evince the reality of a supernatural power at work in the Christian message.

Pascal goes on to point out that the Christian faith has not only changed lives dramatically, freeing people from their bondage to the earth, but has also managed to flourish in the face of all sorts of powerful opposition. With rhetorical verve he writes,

> All the great ones on earth unite, scholars, sages, kings. They write, they condemn, they slay. And, despite opposition from all these quarters, these simple powerless people resist all these powers and bring to their knees even the kings, scholars, sages, and sweep idolatry from the face of the earth. And all this is accomplished by the power which had foretold it. (433)

Although the picture he sketches here is certainly idealized, it nonetheless contains a great deal of truth. Under persecution, the Christian faith indeed has often flourished and even, in the end, prevailed. Surely its success, in even the most difficult of conditions, is a solid mark of its truth, says Pascal.

But we must be very careful about how we understand an argument of this sort. What kind of success can we consider a sign of the truth? Let us look for a moment at the way in which success arguments were deployed by early Christian theologians. Some representative examples can be found, for instance, in that most famous essay written by St. Athanasius in the fourth century, *On the Incarnation of the Word.* Speaking of the extraordinary success of the gospel, St. Athanasius writes,

> For formerly the whole world and every place was led astray by the worshipping of idols, and men regarded nothing else but the idols as gods. But now, all the world over, men are deserting the superstition of the idols, and taking refuge with Christ; and, worshipping him as God, are by his means coming to know that Father also whom they knew not. And, marvelous fact, whereas the objects of worship were various and of vast number, and each place had its own idol, and he who was accounted a god among them had no power to pass over to the neighboring place, so as to persuade those of neighboring peoples to worship him, but was barely served even among his own people; for no one else worshipped his neighbor's god — on the contrary, each man kept to his own idol, thinking it to be lord of all — Christ alone is worshipped as one and the same among all peoples; and what the weakness of the idols could not do — to persuade, namely, even those dwelling close at hand — this Christ has done, persuading not only those close at hand, but simply the entire world, to worship one and the same Lord, and through him God, even his Father. (§46)

Athanasius goes on to press the point further, and asks

> What man's doctrine that ever was has prevailed everywhere, one and the same, from one end of the earth to the other, so that his worship has winged its way through every land? Or why, if Christ is, as they say, a man, and not God the Word, is not his worship prevented by the gods they have from passing into the same land where they are? (§49)

He concludes:

> And, to sum the matter up, behold how the Saviour's doctrine is everywhere increasing, while all idolatry and everything opposed to the faith of Christ is daily dwindling and losing power, and falling. (§55)

This he refers to as "proof of the divinity of the Saviour."

St. Athanasius's assessment of the success of the Christian gospel in the world is quite enthusiastic. Based on what he was saying in the fourth century, I suppose he and his early readers expected something like the universal triumph of the Christian faith in short order. The daily dwindling of other faiths could go on only so long before they would all be extirpated from the face of the earth. But this is not how history has gone. There are still Hindus and Sikhs, Shinto shrines, Buddhist monasteries, Jains, nature religions, and faiths of many other sorts. Since the time of Christ, Islam has arisen and has come to be a world power, operating mainly, however, out of the region of its birth. The success argument, given a purely quantitative twist, is not itself a success, because the Christian gospel has not succeeded in abolishing all other religions. If this is the mark of truth to be expected, it is a mark we must do without.

There is, however, a more subtle rendering of the success argument that does not run aground on contrary facts. It is suggested by some of Athanasius's early remarks. To contrast it with what I have called the quantitative rendering of the success argument, we can refer to it as the qualitative version. So far, the Christian religion is the only religion in human history that has appealed to significant numbers of people in every world culture, has succeeded in changing lives in all times and places, and has managed to have some degree of positive social as well as individual benefits where it has been sincerely embraced. All other religions have been culture-bound, however numerous their adherents. Perhaps only Zen Buddhism has come close to having a universal or nearly universal potential of appeal across cultures, and then only to a fairly rare sort of individual, as mostly a psychological technique, or set of techniques, for producing results within the individual, and not also as a social force for good.

Certainly organizations calling themselves "Christian" have often had deleterious and even disastrous effects on human society. But such movements have clearly diverged at least as far from the gospel of Christ as they have from the restraints of common morality. Sheep ought not to be judged by the actions of wolves who wear wool.

Related to this point, however, there is a serious question. If Christianity is true, as Pascal believed, and it is a mark of its truth, a sign of its supernatural origin and power, that it changes people's lives, then why isn't it a great deal more successful than it is? This is not necessarily to ask why it has not displaced Hinduism altogether, along with all the other faiths, but rather why it has not succeeded more dramatically in transforming the lives of the adherents it does have, or at least that it seems to have?

In note 366, Pascal writes "Two sorts of men in every religion." He follows this with the word "Superstition" and the word "concupiscence." Of course, as a religious person himself,

Pascal does not mean to indicate that there are just two sorts of people in every religion, the superstitious and those who are completely in the grip of their desires, the concupiscent. There are presumably genuinely spiritual people in every major world religious tradition. But in addition to these, there are in every religion people attempting to use religious practices for their own ends. As we are nowadays well aware, charlatans and con artists flock to organized religion in order to exploit the institutions, practices, and, mainly, the tremendous trust to be found there. These are the real wolves in sheep's clothing. A position of leadership in a religious institution is a nearly ideal guise for self-aggrandizing manipulation. Regular association with religious people puts a deceptive soul in touch with trusting individuals who are likely to give another person the benefit of any doubt and so haplessly play into his schemes unaware. It is clear how religion can be a magnet for the unscrupulous. And this is to be regretted. Yet, there is another side to the story. When I was in my early teens, I remember complaining to my father that there seemed to be far too many hypocrites in Christian churches. His response was, "Can you think of a better place for them to be?" Within a religious context it is always possible that their true desires will be eroded by contact with genuinely spiritual people.

In every religion there is another sort of person, a type of person who wants to look out for himself in life and believes that adherence to religious beliefs and engagement in religious practices will magically have a beneficial effect on his fortunes. These are people who are "making a deal with God." In their own way they are exploiting religion for purposes of their own. Not wanting to be transformed, they are hoping that their religious acts will transform life to suit their wishes. This is a slightly more subtle form of concupiscence, desire out of control. Love of God, if it exists in their hearts, is strictly subordinated to love of self. The superstitious are taking no chances. They are careful not to flout any cosmic laws that might be transgressed to their own detriment. And they want to exploit whatever procedures there might be for cheating fate or manipulating the future. In the end their religiosity is just as manipulative as that of the outright scoundrel cloaking himself in the mantle of piety, although it doesn't necessarily affect other people adversely.

It is a traditional Christian belief that God has created us human beings with free will and that he will not decisively override our exercise of our freedom in the formation of our own characters. We freely assent to sin and thus depart from the true spirituality for which we were created. That is to say, we put ourselves first in an extravagant and inappropriate way, and we allow our desires to grow wildly out of our control so that the eventual result of our misuse of our freedom is an unanticipated bondage to the earth and to our desires for what it contains. Christianity offers the true diagnosis of our condition and the path of salvation for its reversal or healing. It does not impose a contrary bondage. True spirituality, genuine religiosity, is always a freely entered state of being. Because God respects our freedom and hence refuses to impose his will unilaterally upon his creatures, the doors are wide open for concupiscence and superstition to enter into religious contexts and flourish there. Because human beings are free — or, better, because in our bondage we have the capacity to resist the truth — there can be no guarantee or even a realistic expectation that the truth about ultimate matters would win the world over if indeed it did enter our realm.

Such realizations as these must temper any appropriate formulation of a success argument for the truth of Christianity. And such reminders will work to block standard objections against the deployment of this sort of argument. I believe that

Pascal's endorsement of a success argument is altogether amenable to these qualifications and restrictions and that it thus should be taken seriously by anyone inquiring sincerely into the truth of the Christian faith.

Christianity claims to offer to us the most complete revelation of God to humankind. It also claims another important exclusivity: the God of Christ is the only God there is, and a proper relation to Christ will ultimately be the only form of a proper relation to God. These are strong claims, and many people with a sensitivity to other world religious traditions have found them objectionable. One line of objection that often is launched by critics consists in pointing out that Christian themes and claims are not utterly unique among world religions and then inferring from that fact that Christianity can make no distinctive claim to truth. Some Old Testament stories are similar to narratives found within other ancient Near Eastern traditions. We now know of Mesopotamian fertility religions that embraced the theme of a dying and rising vegetation god, and such characteristic principles of Christian ethics as the Golden Rule are present in other religious traditions far removed from historical Christian or Jewish influence. Other traditions talk of salvation, enjoin prayer, and tell stories of miraculous events in their histories. Christianity is not utterly unique, despite its claims to exclusivity. This is the conclusion critics often draw. And without any hesitation, they usually then take the further step of dismissing the claim of Christian faith to embrace the one true religion.

The background reasoning seems to be something like this: if Christianity shares ideas with previously existing religious traditions, traditions whose formation was thus independent of the influence of Christianity, then either the Christian faith has borrowed some of its ideas from these other traditions, or these ideas arose independently in the different religions. If

Christians borrowed their ideas from other religions, then their ideas came not from God but from other men and women; they were of human, not divine origin. If on the contrary these ideas developed independently in Christian thought and in the thought of other religions, critics likewise assert that this is a sign that the human mind is their source, not divine revelation. Christians claim that God has revealed to us the correct diagnosis of the human condition, the true path of salvation, and the proper ideal for human life. But if Christian theology seems to be just a pastiche of human thoughts on ultimate matters, there is no reason to think that it, above all other religions, captures the truth on such issues. This is the critic's underlying reasoning, and it is deeply flawed.

In a short, enigmatic note, Pascal writes,

> On the fact that the Christian religion is not unique.
> Far from being a reason for believing it not to be the true religion, it is on the contrary what proves it to be so. (747)

Again, we have an instance of Pascal turning the tables on a critic, taking what is alleged to count against the truth of Christianity as, on the contrary, a sign of its truth.

In our own time the popular Christian writer C. S. Lewis said that if in order to be a Christian he had to deny the existence of truth in all the other great world religions, he could not possibly endorse the Christian faith. What both Lewis and Pascal seem to have had in mind may be something like this: if there is a God who created all human beings for eternal fellowship with their Creator, then it is to be expected that he would have created them all with the capacity to come to know him and that, further, he would in some way make himself available to all, however overtly or subtly. If Christianity is true, then the God who exists is a loving, saving person of perfect goodness, wisdom, and power. And if there is, finally, one and only one way of attaining eternal communion with God from out of our present plight, then we ought to expect at least hints and reverberations of that truth to be made available in this life to all created persons. If in the person of Christ God is reaching out to the world, and if in Christianity we have the most complete revelation of the divine economy of salvation, then we ought to expect tenets of the Christian faith and elements of the Christian story to focus, elaborate, and clarify elements of divine truth to be found worldwide. If Christian teaching were utterly unique, it would be idiosyncratic rather than universal in appeal, and this would be out of step with its own portrayal of a God who loves and seeks to save all the lost. If it is true, the lack of its total uniqueness is to be expected, not looked upon as a problem. It is not a Christian claim that there is no revelation to be found outside the Bible. Quite the contrary. The apostle Paul makes clear that God has never left himself without a witness. Not only is it not incumbent upon a Christian to deny that there is truth outside the church, it is incumbent upon him or her to deny that there is no truth outside the church.

And yet Pascal believed that in virtue of having the purest and most complete revelation from God, the Christian faith is the only world religion that can be judged true *as a whole*. A rational person seeking to follow the path most likely to lead to the full truth available to human beings about ultimate religious matters and most likely to lead to the proper relationship to God, Pascal was convinced, should wager his life on the Christian God.

Distinguishing between Christianity and Islam, Pascal wrote,

It is not by what is obscure in Mahomet, and might be claimed to have a mystical sense, that I want him to be judged, but by what is clear, by his paradise and all the rest. That is

what is ridiculous about him, and that is why it is not right
to take his obscurities for mysteries, seeing that what is clear
in him is ridiculous. It is not the same with Scripture. I admit
that there are obscurities as odd as those of Mahomet, but
some things are admirably clear, with prophecies manifestly
fulfilled. So it is not an even contest. We must not confuse
and treat as equal things which are only alike in their obscurities, and not in the clarity which earns respect for the obscurities. (218)

Pascal obviously lived and wrote in a time before Moslem
leaders issued death sentences against authors who made disparaging remarks about the founder of Islam. The point he was
striving to make was that religions are not all equals. In the
note immediately following, he goes on to say,

Other religions, like those of the heathen, are more popular,
for they consist in externals, but they are not for clever men.
A purely intellectual religion would be more appropriate to
the clever, but would be no good for the people. The Christian
religion alone is appropriate for all, being a blend of external
and internal. (219)

Pascal was convinced that among all the world religions, one
stands out — the Christian religion. It alone has all the marks
of the truth.

A few years ago, a prominent philosopher from another
part of the country visited Notre Dame. After many decades
utterly devoid of any personal religious belief, this man had
undergone a significant life change. In a small gathering, he
was asked by one of our graduate students how it came about.
I am told that in response to this question, he answered that,
at a certain point, he had come to feel a need in his life. Without
any religious convictions of his own, he said, he began to read

all the world's great religious literature — Hindu, Buddhist, Moslem, Jewish, Christian, and so on. After extensive reading, he found himself concluding that some form of Judaism was the truth, either Old Testament Judaism or Christian Judaism. On further reading and reflection, he decided that the truth is to be found foremost in Christian Judaism — that is to say, in the fullness of Christian faith. He became a Christian.

This is exactly the sort of judgment Pascal believed a person would come to if he surveyed all the religious traditions of the world. The truth is to be found foremost and focused in the Christian religion. Or, to put it another way, Pascal seems to have thought that the searching atheist, the inquiring agnostic, would be led to conclude that if there is any God at all, it is the Christian God. And of course the Christian God is the God of the Jews. Thus, the appropriateness of the term "Christian Judaism." The Christian faith builds on the faith of the Jews. It presents itself as the capstone of the Jewish history of dealings with God. And this rooting in Judaism is seen by Pascal as another strand in the overall fabric of evidence pointing in the direction of Christian truth. He perceives the Jews as standing out in interesting ways:

> It is certain that in certain parts of the world we can see a peculiar people, separated from the other peoples of the world, and this is called the Jewish people.
>
> I see then makers of religions in several parts of the world and throughout the ages, but their morality fails to satisfy me and their proofs fail to give me pause. Thus I should have refused alike the Moslem religion, that of China, of the ancient Romans, and of the Egyptians solely because, none of them bearing the stamp of truth more than another, nor anything which forces me to choose it, reason cannot incline towards one rather than another.

But as I consider this shifting and odd variety of customs and beliefs in different ages, I find in one corner of the world a peculiar people, separated from all the other peoples of the earth, who are the most ancient of all and whose history is earlier by several centuries than the oldest histories we have.

I find then this great and numerous people, descended from one man, worshipping one God, and living according to a law which they claim to have received from his hand. They maintain that they are the only people in the world to whom God has revealed his mysteries; that all men are corrupt and in disgrace with God, that they have been abandoned to their senses and their own minds; and that this is the reason for the strange aberrations and continual changes of religions and customs among them, whereas these people remain un-shakeable in their conduct; but that God will not leave the other peoples for ever in darkness, that a Redeemer will come, for all; that they are in the world to proclaim him to men; that they have been expressly created to be the forerunners and heralds of this great coming, and to call all peoples to unite with them in looking forward to this Redeemer.

My encounter with this people amazes me and seems worthy of attention. (454)

And certainly the Jewish people are to be marveled at — dispersed throughout the world and persecuted nearly everywhere, they not only survive but thrive to an unparalleled degree. In nearly every walk of life, in almost every profession in the Western world and on the international scene, Jewish people are disproportionately among the most prominent and accomplished contributors to human culture. It has often been commented that there does seem to be something very special about the Jewish people. From a Pascalian point of view, this is significant, and it points ultimately to the Jews' special calling by God.

This extraordinary context — the history of the Jewish people — is the context within which Christianity arose. This, Pascal believes, merits our attention. He not only finds the many strengths of the Jewish people noteworthy but views even their weaknesses as relevant to the credibility of the religious message they pass on to the world. Consider for example the following note about the Bible:

> *Sincerity of the Jews.* Lovingly and faithfully they hand on this book in which Moses declares that they have been ungrateful towards God throughout their lives, that he knows they will be still more so after his death, but that he calls heaven and earth to witness against them that he told them so often enough.
>
> He declares that God will in the end grow angry with them and disperse them among the peoples of the earth, that as they angered him by worshipping gods that were not their gods, so he will provoke them by calling on a people that is not his people, and he wishes all his words to be preserved eternally and his book to be placed in the ark of the covenant to serve for ever as a witness against them. Isaiah. Isaiah says the same thing, XXX.8. (452)

The Jews, Pascal says, have taken pains to preserve a book that is unflattering to them. This surely merits our attention. They do not present to the world for its acknowledgment a set of documents portraying them in their best light. The presentation and transmission of a positive portrayal could be thoroughly intelligible in purely human terms. But the Jews' preservation and transmission of the documents that make up their scriptures is a different matter altogether. Pascal's reasoning seems to be this: they have not been preserved because they were flattering, so they must have been preserved because they were true and held to be precious as deriving directly from God.

Pascal devotes many pages of his notes to laying out Old Testament prophecies of the coming of the Redeemer, the Christ. This motif of prophecy and fulfillment seems very important to him for its evidentiary value. The events of the New Testament, remarkable in themselves as they are, did not just come to pass; they were foretold hundreds of years in advance. Their occurrence as prophecy fulfillment thus attests to the truth and divine origin of the original prophecy passages.

By directing our attention to considerations of prophecy, understood as predictive of the future, Pascal shows that he writes from a previous century. A great many theologians and biblical scholars of our own time have left behind such categories of thinking as premodern and antiquated. But I believe they have been far too quick in their utter dismissal of this traditionally important category of evidence for the truth of Christianity. We must, however, acknowledge that the use Pascal made of Old Testament prophecy depends on assumptions concerning the original authorship and date of the documents widely controverted among contemporary biblical scholars. And yet, for all the historical care and arduous work displayed by modern biblical studies in the universities, it has often been pointed out by philosophers in recent years that most of this modern scholarship has arrived at results detrimental to traditional handling of biblical texts only by assuming a naturalistic or antisupernaturalistic picture of the world, a worldview, of course, completely biased against any claim to a divine revelation or prophetic intervention into the world of nature. The prophecy-fulfillment motif of biblical interpretation presupposes at least an openness to the possibility of divine inspiration behind the biblical texts. If any such divine origin or influence is ruled out as impossible from the start, it will be very difficult to make a plausible claim concerning Old Testament prophecy of New Testament occurrences. If, however, we try to maintain an open mind concerning the possibility of such divine influence on the human authorship of the biblical documents, we can find much of interest in this category of prophecy that so fascinated Pascal. Reproduction of a longish note in the *Pensées* will give us at least some limited idea of how Pascal used this category:

> *During the lifetime of the Messiah.* A riddle. Ezek. XVII.
> His precursor. Mal. III.
> He will be born a child. Is. IX.
> He will be born in the town of Bethlehem. Mic. V.
> He will mainly appear in Jerusalem and will be born of the family of Judah and David.
> He is to blind the wise and learned. Is. VI, Is. VIII — Is. XXIX — Is. LXI and preach good tidings to the poor and meek, open the eyes of the blind, heal the sick — and lead into light those who languish in darkness. Is. LXI.
> He is to teach the way of perfection and be the teacher of the Gentiles. Is. LV; XLII.1-7.
> The prophecies are to be unintelligible to the ungodly. Dan. XII. — Hos. XIV.9. but intelligible to those who are properly instructed.
> The prophecies which represent him as poor represent him as ruler of the nations: Is. LII.14; LIII, etc. Zech IX.9.
> The prophecies which foretell the time only foretell him as ruler of the Gentiles and suffering, not as in the clouds and a judge. And those which represent him thus as a judge and in glory do not indicate the time.
> That he is to be the victim for the sins of the world. Is. XXXIX, LIII, etc.
> He is to be the precious cornerstone. Is. XXVIII.16.
> He is to be the stone of stumbling and rock of offence. Is. VIII.
> Jerusalem is to dash itself against this stone.

The builders are to reject it. Ps. CXVII.22.

God is to make this stone the head of the corner.

And the stone is to grow into a mighty mountain and fill all the earth. Dan. II.

That he is thus to be rejected, unrecognized, betrayed. Ps. CIX.8. Sold. Zech. XI.12: spat upon, buffeted, mocked, afflicted in countless ways, given gall to drink. Ps. LXIX.21: pierced. Zech. XII.10: his feet and hands pierced, slain and lots cast for his raiment. Ps. XXII.

That he would rise again. Ps. XV. the third day. Hos. VI.2.

That he would ascend into heaven to sit on the right hand. Ps. CX.

That kings would take up arms against him. Ps. II.

That being on the right hand of the Father he would be victorious over his enemies.

That the kings of the earth and all the peoples will worship him. Is. LX.

That the Jews will continue to exist as a nation. Jeremiah.

That they will be wanderers without kings, etc. Hos. III. Without prophets. Amos.

Awaiting salvation and not finding it. Is.

Vocation of the Gentiles through Jesus Christ. Is LII.15. Is. LV — Is. LX — Ps. LXXI.

Hos. 1.9: 'Ye are not my people and I will not be your God, when ye are multiplied by dispersion. In the places were it is said they are not my people, I will call it my people.' (487)

This is just one example of Pascal's interest in prophecy. There are many pages in the *Pensées* that simply reproduce passages from the Old Testament prophets. Pascal obviously thought of this as important. After making a comment about the life of Jesus, in another place, he adds,

And what crowns it all is that it was foretold, so that no one could say it was the effect of chance.

Anyone with only a week to live will not find it in his interest to believe that all this is just a matter of chance.

Now, if we were not bound by our passions, a week and a hundred years would come to the same thing. (326)

In another passage, he even goes so far as to say "The most weighty proofs of Jesus are the prophecies" (335).

Now, why exactly does Pascal consider biblical prophecy to be so important? Anyone can make a lucky guess concerning the future. People do pick winning lottery numbers, despite tremendous odds stacked against them. The local weather forecaster gets it right now and then. Science fiction writers and even cartoonists sometimes write of or represent things that come about after a passage of many years. The world is full of purported psychics making predictions. What in the world would successful prediction or foreshadowing have to do with the integrity of biblical religion or the theological truth of Christianity?

The answer is basically quite simple. A single successful prediction about a remote or unlikely event can be just a lucky guess, a shot in the dark that just happened to hit its target. But the more successful predictions of that sort a person is able to make, the less likely we are to be fully satisfied with just ascribing it all to luck. At a certain point we have to hypothesize some explanation for the success, some connection, mechanism, ability, or power responsible for the otherwise highly improbable accuracy.

Prophecies. If a single man had written a book foretelling the time and manner of Jesus' coming and Jesus had come in conformity with these prophecies, this would carry infinite weight.

But there is much more here. There is a succession of

men over a period of 4,000 years, coming consistently and invariably one after the other, to foretell the same coming; there is an entire people proclaiming it, existing for 4,000 years to testify in a body to the certainty they feel about it, from which they cannot be deflected by whatever threats and persecutions they may suffer. This is of a quite different order of importance. (332)

Even allowing for an overly exuberant statement here, and cutting back on the claimed time span, the point remains that a confluent series of prophecies made by different people at different times and culminating in a single fulfillment by the life of so remarkable a person as Jesus cries out for an explanation of a quite extraordinary sort. Pascal thinks that the most reasonable explanation is that God was involved in the prophecy and fulfillment, thereby giving us an extra ground for accepting Jesus as the culmination of divine revelation.

By what mechanism other than divine revelation could any human being or group of humans reliably foretell extremely unlikely details concerning a future shrouded in obscurity? In my own life I have known a few intelligent, sincere, and completely honest people who claim to have had dreams or visions concerning a very specific and otherwise completely unanticipated event or series of events in their future, a foretelling that they discovered later on had come true in great detail. In reporting to me these unusual occurrences, those who described their state of mind at the time of the dream or vision invariably have spoken of their own involvement in a completely passive way. "A voice spoke to me," or "a vivid dream came to me," or "I saw something, and then it faded." These were not professional psychics or fortune-tellers but ordinary people having an extraordinary experience on one or more occasion. In each case there was no good, plausible naturalistic explanation available. There had been no hints or signs subconsciously processed. And there is no natural mechanism we can reasonably suppose to link the future retrocausally with the present. Each person who has told me of such an experience has, in the process of trying to understand how it possibly could have happened, eventually ascribed it to a divine influence. For, presumably, only a being such as God, whose existence and knowledge is free of those restrictions that bind us to the present moment and the ever-fading past could possibly access and communicate such details from the future to the present. The same considerations that have led so many people with personal glimpses into the future to refer them to God as their source can easily lead readers focusing on prophetic passages in the Bible to see a persuasive case for divine involvement there.

But there is no denying that the academic enterprise of biblical studies has muddied the waters a great deal for anyone interested in considerations of biblical prophecy. By questioning matters of authorship, date, literary intent, and meaning, many critics of the traditional handling of purportedly prophetic passages in the Old Testament documents have made it much more difficult for contemporary people seeking the truth to put the amount of weight on this sort of consideration that Pascal assigned to it.

Pascal would probably criticize the critics, question the questioners, and attack head-on the naturalistic or antisupernaturalistic presuppositions to be found behind so much academic work in biblical studies nowadays. But to try to surmise and represent how that argument might go in detail is beyond our purposes in this chapter. I am seeking only to sketch out the various lines of considerations that Pascal took to be marks of the truth of Christianity. An assessment of the cogency and results of contemporary biblical scholarship is far beyond our purview. However, it is appropriate for me to raise a caveat concerning the recent work that itself would raise a caveat concerning Pascal's argument at this juncture. Any dismissal of the possibility of prophecy based solely on an antisupernatural bias may itself deserve to be dismissed by people seeking to discover what the truth might be concerning ultimate issues regarding the supernatural. And yet, because of the complex historical controversies in the neighborhood, we will probably come to find other categories of evidence brought to our attention by Pascal to be more persuasive.

Pascal believed that there were, in the life and teachings of Jesus, many marks of his extraordinary status. For example, he writes,

> *Proofs of Jesus Christ.* Jesus said great things so simply that he seems not to have thought about them, and yet so clearly that it is obvious what he thought about them. Such clarity together with such simplicity is wonderful. (309)

And, he adds later, "never before or since has any man come who taught anything nearly as divine as this" (325). Pascal views the nature of Jesus' teaching as a mark of his divinity.

Another mark is provided by the miracles he performed. Throughout the centuries, the miracles of Jesus have been seen as an important part of the case to be made for his divinity. But, like the category of prophecy, the category of miracle has been viewed with suspicion by many people in the modern world. In the eighteenth century, the Scottish philosopher David Hume defined a miracle as a violation of a law of nature and argued, on the basis of his definition, that, for all the accounts of miracles we have, it is always more probable that the miracle story is false than that a law of nature was violated. Hume believed that we come to call a conviction we have about how nature works "a law of nature" only after we have the weightiest evidence that this is in fact the way things always go. Thus, Hume thought, it is impossible to have more evidence for some alleged violation of a law than for the law itself. A law of nature can be thought of as a claim of the form "Whenever something has characteristic (or is in state) *A,* then it has property (or is in state) *B*" or of the form "Whenever event *C* occurs, event *E* results." A miracle, then, will be a case in which some *A* is not accompanied by the requisite *B* or in which some *C* does not cause its customary effect *E.* But, Hume points out, any evidence that *A* is always joined to *B* or that *C* always results in *E* stands as evidence against the reliability of any claim to have witnessed *A* without *B* or *C* without *E.* Thus, once something is established as a law, we cannot expect to be in a position to have good evidence that a violation of it has occurred. And without good evidence for a miracle, there cannot be reasonable belief in the miracle story. Thus, followers of Hume have concluded, it is impossible to hold a reasonable belief that any miracle has ever occurred.

Some people influenced by Hume have gone so far as to call miracles "impossible." They say that laws of nature tell us how nature works, and since to claim a miracle is to say that nature has not worked in the way in which nature works, it is to claim an impossibility. Others say that a belief in miracles is not scientifically respectable. A scientific worldview, they say, assumes that everything natural has a regular, natural cause. To think otherwise is to give up science. So, they conclude, any belief in miracles is unscientific, even antiscientific.

Hume's critique of miracles, and the legacy it has left to the modern world, has been enormously influential. Many sincere students of the Bible have tried to read around the miracle stories because of it and have exerted themselves to come up with a version of Christian faith devoid of belief in the miraculous. But all of this is unnecessary. For Hume has had numerous critics himself who have pointed to any number of weaknesses in his argument, the assumptions behind it, and the way it has been appropriated by followers.

I have just sketched one facet of the Humean reasoning. No more is needed for our purposes. From a Pascalian point of view Hume is wrong from the start, from his very conception of miracle. Pascal, and along with him most every careful Christian thinker, defines a miracle not as a violation of a law of nature but rather as an event exceeding the natural powers of the created objects involved in it. If we want to think in terms of laws of nature, we can say that a miracle *surpasses* rather than *violates* them. Suppose it is a law that "wherever *A* then *B*." The theist always understands laws as restricted to the natural domain, so a full explication of such a law should properly state that "wherever *A*, and nothing in addition to *A*, then *B*," or "wherever *A*, and God does not intervene to the contrary, *B*." But in a miracle God does intervene, producing effects that exceed the powers of natural objects alone. So no natural law is violated. Its implicit independence condition is just not satisfied, so it is not in effect. Natural laws thus do not present us with "the way nature works," *simpliciter;* they just describe the way nature works when God is not introducing an exceptional development for his own purposes. Perhaps another way to put it is this: God creates objects with powers. Natural laws tell us what happens when those objects act in accordance with their own powers. In a miracle, divine power produces an event beyond what is within the natural powers of the objects involved to produce. There is no contradiction, no impossibility. And there is no reason to believe that there cannot be good evidence for the occurrence of such an event or good grounds for accepting one to have occurred.

Pascal thus takes the miracle stories of the New Testament seriously and recommends them as important signs of the truth. He is aware that there are many false stories of miracles and that because of them many cautious people hesitate to accept the truth of any miracle account whatsoever. But to that worry he has an interesting, and characteristically clever, reply. Consider medicine and pseudomedicine:

> After considering what makes us trust impostors claiming to have cures, to the extent that we often put our lives into their hands, it seemed to me that the real reason is that some of them are genuine, for there could not possibly be so many false ones, enjoying so much credit, unless some of them were genuine. If there had never been a cure for any ill, and all ills had been incurable, men could not possibly have imagined that they could provide any, still less could so many others have given credence to those who boasted of having such cures. Similarly, if a man boasted that he could prevent death, no one would believe him, because there is no example of that happening. (734)

Applying this to the case of miracles, he reasons,

> Thus instead of concluding that there are no true miracles because there are so many false ones, we must on the contrary say that there certainly are true miracles since there are so many false ones, and that false ones are only there because true ones exist. (734)

Pascal thinks we have very good reason to believe that the miracles reported in the New Testament are genuine. The documents of the New Testament present an unusual kind of history, in many ways. For one thing, those who reported the occurrences were prepared to be put to death for believing them. Says Pascal,

> I only believe histories whose witnesses are ready to be put to death. (822)

This is hyperbolic, of course, but it does make an important point. Whenever witnesses to an event are so sure of their story and of its importance that they will not retract their testimony even under credible threats of death and actual execution, we certainly do take note. And we are hard put to impugn their testimony without extremely good independent reason to do so. But this is precisely what was true of those who have reported to the world the deeds of Jesus. They all lived under persecution and threats of death, and many were martyred for their beliefs. Surely their testimony to miraculous acts on the part of Jesus should be taken very seriously.

Pascal thinks that the Gospel writers have given us a portrait of a man that is noteworthy in many respects. He at one point asks

> Who taught the evangelists the qualities of a perfectly heroic soul, so that they could depict one so perfectly in Jesus? Why do they make him weak in his agony? Do they not know how to describe a steadfast death? Yes, because the same St Luke describes the death of St Stephen more heroically than that of Jesus.
>
> They make him capable of fear before death had become inevitable and then absolutely steadfast.
>
> But when they show him so distressed it is when he distresses himself; when men distress him he is steadfast. (316)

The extraordinary New Testament picture of Jesus does not look like the contrivance of his very ordinary followers. It is too different from what would be expected of triumphalist propaganda. It bears the marks of truth.

The miracle stories are parts of these accounts, continuous with the flow of the whole, and partaking of the credibility of their context. They are thus to be taken very seriously.

And of course the most extraordinary miracle story of all is the story of the resurrection of Jesus from death, told in various ways by different biblical authors. The apostles, the chief followers of Jesus, who had been so stunned and broken by his execution, were a short time later boldly proclaiming that God had raised him from death, in vindication of his special status and mission. They claimed that he had appeared to them over a period of weeks, had walked and eaten with them, had cast away all their doubts, and had given them special instruction for the furtherance of his work. Is their testimony to such a stunning event, or set of events, credible? Pascal wants us to realize that if we reject their testimony, we are stuck with a quite unsatisfying dilemma. He puts it like this: if we were to suppose that their reports are false, we would have to conclude that

> The Apostles were either deceived or deceivers. Either supposition is difficult, for it is not possible to imagine that a man has risen from the dead.
> While Jesus was with them he could sustain them, but afterwards, if he did not appear to them, who did make them act? (322)

If what the apostles reported about Jesus was false, then either they believed it and so were themselves deceived or they knew it was false and so were just deceivers. How plausible is either of these alternatives?

First, consider the claim that the followers of Jesus were themselves deceived, wrongly believing in his miracles and resurrection when no such things had ever actually happened. On this supposition they were themselves just mistaken. But there is something interesting about the concept of a mistake. I can be walking down the street and think I see an old friend approaching but on getting closer realize that I have made a mistake. I can mistakenly believe that today is Saturday when it's Friday. I can make some pretty big mistakes. We all can. But a mistake can only be so big. I cannot mistakenly think I see exactly 419 pink and purple elephants outside my office window, suspended in mid-air. I can't mistakenly think I have twelve arms.

The apostles reported detailed encounters with the risen Christ sometime after his death and burial. Would it have made much sense for loved ones to respond to such reports by saying, "Calm down, dear. It was just your imagination"? Pascal says that it is not possible to imagine that a man has risen from the dead. That's too extreme to be a mistake. And there were no cultural expectations in first-century Judaism that a single man might be raised from the grave by God into a new, yet recognizable, form of life. Hallucination is not plausible. Repeated, convergent mass hallucinations are even less plausible, *much* less plausible. Pascal finds this suggestion absolutely incredible, strictly speaking.

So what of the other possibility? If the testimony of the apostles is false, and it is utterly implausible to think of all of them as deceived by appearances concerning such extraordinary events, then the other possibility, as Pascal points out, is that they never believed for a minute these stories they told about Jesus but were themselves just deceivers. How credible is this supposition? In another passage Pascal writes,

> *Proofs of Jesus Christ.* The hypothesis that the Apostles were knaves is quite absurd. Follow it out to the end and imagine these twelve men meeting after Jesus' death and conspiring to say that he had risen from the dead. This means attacking all the powers that be. The human heart is singularly susceptible to fickleness, to change, to promises, to bribery. One of

them had only to deny his story under these inducements, or still more because of possible imprisonment, tortures and death, and they would all have been lost. Follow that out. (310)

Lying is hard work. When you tell a lie, you don't have reality to back you up. When you tell a lot of lies, one building on the next, you get yourself in an even worse fix. Such deceit requires extraordinary powers of memory as well as imagination. Most of us have a hard enough time remembering things that have actually happened. And when we forget, we can usually rely upon the fact that the truth leaves traces of itself behind — footprints, documents, memory impressions in other people's minds. But when we concoct an alternate reality, a history contrary to what really has happened, we have only our own memories to rely on concerning what we said happened.

A conspiracy of lies is even more fragile. This is from the beginning an exceedingly odd sort of agreement — a number of different people get together, concoct a story, and agree to lie about it, each promising not to break and tell the truth. It is crucial to their agreement that they're all liars, but how in the world can you trust liars to keep their end of an agreement? Any supposition that the apostles of Christ met after his death and entered into this sort of agreement is especially hard to swallow. Here a number of ordinary men from walks of life in which the truth mattered, who had just spent an extended period of time with a charismatic leader whom most non-Christians recognize as one of the greatest moral teachers in history, are supposed to have met together after the death of their leader and, to further his work, agreed to tell outrageous lies about him? This is just too bizarre. And worse, Pascal points out, from these lies they would have had little to gain and much to lose, as circumstances developed. Only one of them need have cracked and the whole conspiracy would have unraveled. And each of them, knowing that each of the others was lying against the grain of his own personality, would surely have suspected that one of the others would crack, and so would have been all the more prepared himself to tell the truth and cut his losses, distancing himself from the others in times of increasing pressure and persecution. Further, recall that we are talking about a message that itself emphasized the importance of walking in the truth. The hypothesis that the followers of Christ were just deceivers is far too out of step with everything we know about them, about their circumstances, about their message, and about human psychology.

But if neither the supposition that the original witnesses whose testimony we have about Christ were deceived nor the hypothesis that they were deceivers is plausible, we must reject the assumption that alone would saddle us with this choice — the claim that their accounts of the deeds of Christ are false. That is to say, any reason we have to believe that they were neither deceived nor deceivers is a reason to accept their testimony, miracle accounts and all, as true. And if the life of Christ was characterized by such extraordinary events as calming a storm with a word, healing a man born blind, feeding a multitude with only a few pieces of food, healing others with a command or a touch, even saving them from death, and being himself raised and transformed after his own execution, we certainly have many marks of his special status and mission with which to reckon.

Throughout the history of Christian thought, the miracles of Christ have often been pointed to as signs of the truth of Christian theology and, particularly, of the truth of its claims about the divinity of Christ, the claims that he came among us from the side of God as one person in two natures, human and divine. But what exactly is the connection between a remarkable act and a reliable assertion? Why should astonishing events such as miracles lead us to accept theological claims?

If in order to make sense of these events, if in order to explain how in the world they could have occurred, we find ourselves having to attribute to Jesus power or knowledge beyond the reach of human nature, so far as we can see, and if a distinctively theological interpretation of those acts makes the best sense of their context as well as the content of the teaching of the person who performed them, then we are justified in taking them as evidence for the truth of the distinctively theological claims that best explain them — that Jesus was in especially close touch with the resources of power and knowledge distinctive of deity or even that he was in some way himself divine.

For many years I did not myself understand how exactly miracles were supposed to function as marks of divine truth, until I met a most extraordinary man. I was living in a vacation house out in the woods on seven acres of land with two other graduate students during my first semester at Yale. A man from the adjoining property introduced himself one day and told me that the night before we had moved in, he had found a motorcycle gang camped in the woods between our houses. It was three A.M., he said, when he appeared among them and persuaded them to leave. He explained that he often roamed the woods at night and hunted when he couldn't sleep because of old war injuries. Unzipping his windbreaker, he showed me the .44 magnum long-barreled handgun in a shoulder holster he always carried with him. "Sometimes makes the folks at the bank a little nervous," he added with a smile and a wink.

Subsequent visits and inquiries on my part led to some war stories that were definitely movie material. He was in a special unit trained in all the relevant martial arts. He could kill at a distance with any projectile — a ballpoint pen, a number two pencil. He and a Shoshone Indian were the only members of

his unit to make it back from the Second World War. And that
was after he had been shot by a tank. I was invited to feel the
hole in this bear-of-a-man's shoulder, while the stories grew in
drama. Jumping from planes behind enemy lines, slitting open
German attack dogs mid-leap, capturing and eliminating Nazi
officers with piano wire. The strategies, the close calls, the
exciting escapes. Better than in the movies. One day I saw a
medallion on the front bumper of his pickup truck inscribed
with the name of a town in Connecticut and "Honorary Police
Chief." I asked about this.

"Oh, it was nothin', Tom. I was just drivin' down the street
one day a few years ago and I see out behind a building four
guys beatin' up some cop they had on the ground. Well, I
couldn't let that happen, so I got outa the truck and stopped
it. The mayor thought it was nice of me to help out, so he
made me honorary chief of police."

I asked, "What happened to the four guys?" He replied,
"Let's just say they had a nice long stay in the hospital."

The stories got more elaborate, and I began to wonder
whether they could possibly all be true. We had gone far beyond
any of the war and spy stories I had ever heard or seen on the
big screen. At a certain point, anyone would become unsure
that all this could possibly be true.

Then, one day, sitting on an outdoor deck playing my
guitar, I was stung by the largest, most menacing-looking wasp
I had ever seen. The sting was extremely painful and the spot
on my left calf immediately began to redden and swell. I became
dizzy. Within a minute or two I couldn't walk. The pain was
terrible, the swelling was huge, and a housemate had to prac-
tically carry me over to the neighbor's for a ride to the hospital.
Upon opening his back door, he looked at my face and said,
"My God, Tom, what's wrong with you?" We explained quickly
as he ushered us into his house.

"Sit down," he said, motioning to an armchair beside us in the den. I did, with pain. I expected him to get his keys, but instead he looked me in the eyes and said, "Now, don't worry about a thing. I'm going to have to do something to help you out, but you may not want to watch." I did want to watch. I'm a philosopher. I'm incurably curious. "We've got to stretch out your leg," he said as he pulled it by the foot, lifting it and propping it up on his own knee as he squatted in front of me. He then joined his two burly hands, thumbs sticking up, and with a sudden, violent motion, crammed them into the back of my left knee, hitting it so hard I thought I was going to see my kneecap bounce off the ceiling (and only this year, sixteen years later, have I had a little trouble with that knee). He then raked his thumbs down the length of my calf, hard, two or three times. Then he looked up and said, "Stand up. You should be fine within a couple of minutes."

I stood up, unassisted, with almost no pain. I put weight on the leg, testing it. No pain. I looked down and was shocked to see that the swelling was almost gone, a little bump where a large egg-sized hill had been. "You OK?" he asked. I was OK, and so were all his stories.

"How did you do that?" I asked. He said, "Oh, it's just a little trick we needed when guys would get screwed up from night jumps. We had to be able to fix anything." From that time on I ceased to doubt any of his stories, however dramatic.

And not too long afterward, I realized that there was a connection between how the events of that afternoon had enhanced the credibility of all his extraordinary stories and how miracles were supposed to do the same for Jesus' teaching and for the extraordinary claims about him made by early Christians. Remarkable actions corroborate remarkable stories. If, in order to explain some astonishing deed, you have to postulate that a person is in touch with some source of knowledge and power far beyond the ordinary, and it is just some such rare status that would be needed to render the claims about that person credible, then witnessing that deed or hearing about it from some very trustworthy source can serve to raise the credibility of the stories, even to the point of banishing all practical doubt. This is what happened with me and my neighbor, and it is just what Pascal was convinced could happen with our judgment about Jesus. If we could come to see the biblical authors as trustworthy witnesses who were willing to lay their lives on the line for the truth of their stories, then we could accept the miracle accounts and, accepting them, accept the distinctive status of Jesus in the divine economy of revelation and salvation.

Pascal believed that when we take the New Testament portrayal of Jesus seriously, we find many strands of evidence for his unique status. A central strand not to be overlooked is a line of thought developed in a very Pascalian spirit by the late C. S. Lewis. Lewis was tired of hearing his fellow intellectuals refer to Jesus as a great moral teacher while dismissing with contempt the central Christian claim that he was literally God Incarnate, Lord of the universe.

Reflecting the logic of Pascal's argument for the reliability of the apostolic witness, Lewis pointed to Jesus' self-presentation in the pages of the New Testament. In many ways — some subtle, some less so — Jesus presented himself as standing in a unique relationship to God the Father, as having divine prerogatives, as having a divine status. He did not ever say, "I am God." In first-century Jewish culture, anyone who said that would not be around very long to say anything else. Blasphemy. And in our own culture, if someone were to say that, I doubt we would take seriously anything else he said. Insanity. But Jesus presented himself in so many ways as divine, forgiving sins (the province of God alone), saying such things as "Before Abraham was, I am," characterizing his own life in terms of the prophecies of the scriptures. So, Lewis argued, he presented himself as God. Now, given this, there are only three possibilities.

First, let us see what follows if we suppose that his self-presentation was wrong, that in fact he was not God. Either he realized the real truth about himself or he did not. If he was not God and knew he was not, yet presented himself as such, then, Lewis says, he was a liar — a deceiver of the worst sort. He asked people to leave their old lives behind and follow him. He called on other human beings to make great sacrifices in his name. If he knew that all this was being built on a complete fabrication, with which he was luring people and leading them on, then he was a liar of the most monstrous kind, ruining the lives of his poor victims for what he knew to be false.

But how plausible is this? If Jesus is acknowledged as one of the greatest moral teachers in history, how could we possibly endorse the hypothesis that he built everything on the most outrageous lie imaginable? This seems utterly preposterous.

The other possibility, however, on the assumption that his self-presentation was false, is the hypothesis that he sincerely believed this falsehood and so was not himself a culpable deceiver after all. He was just mistaken about his own identity. But recall the point made earlier about the concept of a mistake. A student can mistakenly believe that he or she is the smartest person in the class. Perhaps a student can even reasonably yet mistakenly believe that he is the smartest or most musically talented or most athletically accomplished person ever to have attended his university. But the student could not reasonably but mistakenly believe that he was himself God Incarnate. That's just too big for a mistake. We can only get so far off the beam before we're totally in the dark. If Jesus was not divine, but had so distorted a self-image as to think he was divine, especially in the strictly monotheistic context of first-century Judaism, then he was, Lewis says, on a par with a man who

believes he is a boiled egg. In other words, he would have left
the realm of megalomania far behind for the netherworld of
sheer insanity. On this hypothesis, Lewis says, Jesus would have
been a lunatic, plain and simple.

But this is also grossly out of line with the powerful picture
we have of Jesus in the New Testament and with the acceptance
of him as a great moral teacher. It was no lunatic who gave the
Sermon on the Mount, who served his own disciples, who
reached out to the downtrodden, and who taught enduringly
deep truths about genuine humanness. This supposition too is
utterly incredible.

But those are the only possibilities available to us if his
self-presentation was false. Either he knew, in which case he
was a liar, or he did not know, in which case he was a lunatic.
To avoid this dilemma, it suffices to deny the supposition from
which it arises, the hypothesis that his self-presentation was
indeed false. But to deny that offending hypothesis is just to
admit that his self-presentation must have been true, which is
to admit that he is, after all, Lord of the world. "Liar, Lunatic,
Lord": the argument presenting these three possibilities is often
known as the Lewis Trilemma, because initially someone who
is not already a Christian can, on careful reflection, find all
three conclusions objectionable. Lewis wants us to endorse the
least rationally objectionable, what he considers the most evidentially plausible, the conclusion rooted in taking the self-
presentation of Jesus to have been both sincere and sane, the
conclusion in line with all the other strands of evidence we
have surveyed, the conclusion that Jesus was and is the Christ,
the Messiah, the Savior of humankind, the chief revelation of
God to men and women, the Lord of us all. And this is the
conclusion Pascal thought we would be led to if we followed
all the clues we have, if we attended to all the marks of the
truth to be found in our world.

10

FAITH AND THE HEART

I HAVE heard Pascal called "an irrationalist" and contemptu-
ously dismissed as "a mystic" by people who had heard of
his "Night of Fire" experience, who misunderstood his famous
wager argument, and who were ignorant of his concern for
evidence. Pascal is often thought an enemy of reason by those
who believe in nothing other than reason. But by now it should
be becoming quite clear that he was a person with great respect
for the role of reason in human life but who nonetheless recognized that reason has its limits.

After going to great pains to lay out the various lines of
evidence he saw as available for anyone seeking to know the
truth about such ultimate matters as the theological claims
made by Christianity, Pascal expressed his overall view of the
evidential situation by writing that

> The prophecies, even the miracles and proofs of our religion,
> are not of such a kind that they can be said to be absolutely
> convincing, but they are at the same time such that it cannot
> be said to be unreasonable to believe in them. There is thus
> evidence and obscurity, to enlighten some and obfuscate
> others. But the evidence is such as to exceed, or at least equal,

the evidence to the contrary, so that it cannot be reason that decides us against following it, and can therefore only be concupiscence and wickedness of heart. Thus, there is enough evidence to condemn and not enough to convince, so that it should be apparent that those who follow it are prompted to do so by grace and not by reason, and those who evade it are prompted by concupiscence and not by reason. (835)

I believe this is a very important passage for understanding Pascal and for understanding the challenge we face when we confront these ultimate issues. It contains three themes: (1) the balance of the evidence, (2) the role of grace in the lives of those who follow the Christian way, and (3) the role of concupiscence in the lives of those who evade it. Grace is thought of, roughly, as the free and unmerited act of reaching out to us on the part of God. It is a supernatural influence calling us or drawing us to God, at work in the deepest recesses of our personalities if we choose to allow it to work in us. Concupiscence is just the Pascalian category for desire out of control, ministering to the insatiable wants of the self-absorbed ego. The idea is that once we break free of God, we fall into a state of no longer having our desires properly controlled or constrained for our own genuine personal fulfillment. Seeking to govern our own lives, we become governed by them. Choosing control over our own desires, we are controlled by them.

Pascal believes that the evidence available in our world for the truth of Christian theology is at least as good as any evidence that seems to exist to the contrary. But he also judges that the evidence is not such as to be able to compel us in either direction. Those who move away from God do so because of concupiscence. Those who move toward God do so as a response to the call of grace. Marks of the truth are all around us, sufficient to support the life of faith from a rational perspective but insufficient to arrest those who do not seek to know.

But if this is all that can be said for the evidence, what is the point of bringing it to our attention? Why does Pascal dwell so much on the evidence and exercise himself in such clever argumentation? Well, for one thing, by so doing he is clearing away unnecessary obstacles to faith. The various intellectual difficulties or perplexities that pose obstacles to our heeding the call of God must be removed from the path of people who are stumbling over them so that the real nature of the decision to be made will be clear: either to aspire toward finding and following God or to live in this world out of one's own resources alone. This is the negative task that evidential and philosophical argumentation can perform, a sort of ground-clearing enterprise. But there is a more positive task as well.

According to the Bible itself, we are to love God with all our *minds.* Religious faith is not to be compartmentalized, segregated from the life of the intellect. Pascal shows us how a Christian can respond to God with his mind. Christianity is not just a matter of the intellect, a philosophy of life, but it does require us to use our minds to our greatest ability. We can do that only as we think through the problems that trouble us and focus our attention on all the marks of the truth that are available to us.

But just as scrutinizing the evidence is not sufficient for coming to be a Christian, neither is it strictly necessary for Christian faith. We who are intellectually inclined put a high value on evidence and argument, but Pascal says,

> Do not be astonished to see simple people believing without argument. God makes them love him and hate themselves. He inclines their hearts to believe. We shall never believe,

with an effective belief and faith, unless God inclines our hearts, and we shall believe as soon as he does so. (380)

When Pascal speaks here of God making simple people "hate themselves," I believe he is most charitably to be read as indicating that God causes them to hate their selfishness, the tendency in the self to isolation and self-aggrandizement. I'll say more about this in the next chapter. Here I want to focus on Pascal's acknowledgment that religious belief can come about wholly without the benefit of philosophical argument and the marshaling of evidence. This is not to deny, however, that such activity can play a crucial contributory role in the faith of a great many intelligent people who are so constituted that without it they could not believe, either at all, or at least in the full integrity of their personalities. Not everyone has the evidential itch, but for those who do, the means for scratching it is available. And this is important for those to whom it matters. In an interesting passage, Pascal writes,

> Ordinary people have the ability not to think about things they do not want to think about. 'Do not think about the passages concerning the Messiah,' said the Jew to his son. Our own people often behave like this, and this is how false religions are preserved, and even the true one as far as many people are concerned.
>
> But there are some without this ability to stop themselves from thinking, who think all the more for being forbidden to do so. These people rid themselves of false religions, and even of the true one, unless they find solid arguments for them. (815)

Good reasons, solid arguments, and persuasive evidence can play a crucial supporting role for genuine faith in the lives of many people. And Pascal wants to provide for these people. A good relation to God is too important to be missed because of intellectual difficulties that could be dealt with or because of a lack of evidence that could be provided.

And yet, Pascal is always keen to remind us, the name of the game is not satisfying intellectual curiosity, a point he makes quite vividly in this passage:

> This religion so great in miracles, in men holy, pure and irreproachable, in scholars, great witnesses and martyrs, established kings — David — Isaiah, a prince of the blood; so great in knowledge, after displaying all its miracles and all its wisdom, rejects it all and says that it offers neither wisdom nor signs, but only the Cross and folly.
>
> For those who by this wisdom and these signs have deserved your trust, and who have proved their character, declare to you that none of this can change us and make us capable of knowing and loving God, except the virtue contained in the folly of the Cross, without wisdom or signs, and not the signs without this virtue.
>
> Thus our religion is foolish judged by its effective cause, and wise judged by the wisdom which prepares for it. (291)

And this brings us back to Jesus and Nicodemus. The ultimate religious issue for any human being concerns not the drawing of conclusions but the ordering of one's life in one way rather than another. Can we follow the supreme sacrifice of Christ on the cross and sacrifice our self-governance, putting aside concupiscence and opening ourselves to the will of God? What can seem nothing but foolishness to the self-interested ego that calls the shots and deems conduct reasonable or foolish is what is required. No self can be saved that is not given up. But this is a theme we have yet to develop. According to Pascal, the point to remember is that with all the evidence and argument,

we are not yet at the heart of the matter, which is a matter of
the heart:

> The heart has its reasons of which reason knows nothing: we
> know this in countless ways.
>
>   I say that it is natural for the heart to love the universal
> being or itself, according to its allegiance, and it hardens itself
> against either as it chooses. You have rejected one and kept
> the other. Is it reason that makes you love yourself? (423)

Is the heart centered in the self, or does it reach toward God
in humility and love? Is self-interest our chief interest, or can
we transcend that and open our lives up to "the universal
being"?

We come here to an important juncture in Pascal's thought
and to a fundamental conception that will help us to understand what Christian faith is, or at least what it is supposed to
be. Of course faith is a much-revered and much-maligned
concept. H. L. Mencken once said that "Faith may be defined
briefly as an illogical belief in the occurrence of the improbable." But it was Mark Twain who gave the definition most
beloved of critics when he reported the view that "Faith is
believing what you know ain't so." To put it simply, this is a
view of faith as irrational belief, belief that is against reason,
against the evidence, contrary to what we know to be so. From
a Pascalian point of view, this is a complete misrepresentation
of the nature of faith.

Ambrose Bierce, a contemporary of Mark Twain, defined
it like this: "Faith. Belief without evidence in what is told by
one who speaks without knowledge, of things without parallel."
Others have characterized it, in a similar spirit, as "a leap in
the dark" and as "a desperate hope the mind cannot support."
This is a view of faith as nonrational belief, a conception which

allows that, while faith may not be belief in what we know to be false, it is belief that cannot be supported by anything we know. This again, Pascal would insist, is a complete misunderstanding.

First of all, Pascal sees faith and reason as neither inimical nor isolated from one another. To suppose otherwise is an egregious source of error for both these sorts of conception. Second, there is an even deeper error running through all these definitions of faith. They all present faith as being nothing other than belief of a certain sort. But this is far too thin and misleading an account of the central religious disposition in this life. Faith is not a mere species of belief.

Pascal puts it like this:

> It is the heart which perceives God and not the reason. That is what faith is: God perceived by the heart, not by the reason. (424)

Again, this contrast of faith and reason in Pascal is not meant to indicate that the two are inconsistent or that they are autonomous one from the other. The point is that there is no intellectual bridge to be built to God, the crossing of which in the mind's eye counts as faith. Faith is not a deliverance of the reason. It is a matter of the heart.

In talking of the heart, Pascal of course is not engaging in some strange thoracic approach to theology. He is just appropriating an ancient image, prominent in the Bible as in much other great world literature. In referring to the heart, Pascal means to draw our attention to something central, something at the core of the human person, the deepest source or wellspring of beliefs, attitudes, and emotions we have. There are numerous clues throughout his notes concerning what he means. He doesn't mention the heart only in connection with matters of religion. It figures prominently in his response to general skepticism concerning human knowledge claims. Consider, for example, this passage:

> We know the truth not only through our reason but also through our heart. It is through the latter that we know first principles, and reason, which has nothing to do with it, tries in vain to refute them. The sceptics have no other object than that, and they work at it to no purpose. We know that we are not dreaming, but, however unable we may be to prove it rationally, our inability proves nothing but the weakness of our reason, and not the uncertainty of all our knowledge, as they maintain. For knowledge of first principles, like space, time, motion, number, is as solid as any derived through reason, and it is on such knowledge, coming from the heart and instinct, that reason has to depend and base all its argument. (110)

In the same note, he goes on later to say,

> Our inability must therefore serve only to humble reason, which would like to be the judge of everything, but not to confute our certainty. As if reason were the only way we could learn! Would to God, on the contrary, that we never needed it and knew everything by instinct and feeling! But nature has refused us this blessing, and has instead given us only very little knowledge of this kind; all other knowledge can be acquired only through reasoning. (110)

And he finally concludes,

> That is why those to whom God has given religious faith by moving their hearts are very fortunate, and feel quite legitimately convinced, but to those who do not have it we can only give such faith through reasoning, until God gives it by

moving their heart, without which faith is only human and useless for salvation. (110)

Without certain basic principles, reason cannot function. When we compile evidence and draw conclusions, we are assuming certain principles concerning what counts as evidence, assuming certain forms of reasoning to be reliable, and assuming the general reliability of at least some of our basic experience of the world. These principles cannot be evidentially endorsed or logically guaranteed by reason. We cannot prove them correct. And yet we cannot live without them. We do accept them. But why? Pascal seems to believe that everything that is most important in life is known through the heart, through what he also calls "instinct" or "feeling."

The heart is the deepest point of contact for emotions, attitudes, and beliefs. It is also the deepest source for human actions. Faith, says Pascal, is God perceived by the heart. What does that mean? We are dealing here with a difficult metaphor. What is the difference between perception by the heart and perception by the eyes? Well, for one thing, perception by the eyes is contact with reality through only one modality of human connectedness. Perception by the mind might be just as limited. Perception by the heart is presumably more complex, more multiform, and also deeper. It may involve connectedness that is mental (intellectual), attitudinal (emotional), and volitional (involved with will and action) and thus, in its completeness, spiritual.

What exactly does it mean for the heart to perceive God? This may happen if and when a person is moving his or her life God-ward, in the direction of the divine, seeking a knowledge and love of God, longing for communion with God, and seeing all the world by the light of this movement. Perhaps this is all connected profoundly with Pascal's Wager. To wager on

God is to want there to be a God, to hope there is a God, to direct one's life in such a way that if there is a God, then one can come to know God. I don't want to say that perceiving God with the heart is the same thing as wagering on God, but determined wagering may be at least a prolegomenon to faith, or even a beginning, early form of faith. In the passage just cited, Pascal talks of giving faith through reasoning, a form of faith he admits is "only human." What does he mean by this? He has already conceded that the evidences for the truth of Christianity are not such as to compel belief. But he may think of the entirety of his reasoning — reasoning about religious indifference, the inevitability of death, the necessity for finding meaning, the vanity of life in this world without God, the marks of Christian truth, and the reasoning of the Wager argument — as sufficient to move a rational, unbiased person toward seeking in the God-ward direction. And if all that reasoning does succeed in changing people's lives by changing what they think and how they live, that will be a change for the good, preparing them for a change from God.

Most days I know that the sun is up not by seeing it in the sky but by seeing everything else in its light. Perhaps the life of faith should be modeled on this. Or at least it may be that one way of knowing God does not require a direct apprehension of the divine in any one sensory mode. That is, after all, only the most minimal way in which we know things in this world. Perhaps there is a way of knowing God that consists, at least in part, in seeing everything else in the light of God. Granted, we are still in the realm of metaphor here, but I hope it is an illuminating metaphor. At least, this may be a way of having faith, however human a way. It becomes divine as the openness to God it creates allows God's grace to penetrate the deepest recesses of the personality — the heart — and effect genuine, full-bodied saving faith, the perception of God by the heart.

This is what Jesus called being "born anew" in his encounter with Nicodemus (John 3:3, RSV).

Christian faith is connected with hope, desire, and action. It is also connected with belief. The more mature the faith, the more mature the belief with which it is connected. Faith is not the same thing as belief, if by belief we mean mental assent. Faith is much more. It is a form of life. And this form of life involves important habits — habits of thought and desire and action. In a very important passage, Pascal says,

> For we must make no mistake about ourselves: we are as much automaton as mind. As a result, demonstration is not the only instrument for convincing us. How few things can be demonstrated! Proofs only convince the mind; habit provides the strongest proofs and those that are most believed. It inclines the automaton, which leads the mind unconsciously along with it. Who ever proved that it will dawn tomorrow, and that we shall die? And what is more widely believed? . . . In short, we must resort to habit once the mind has seen where the truth lies, in order to steep and stain ourselves in that belief which constantly eludes us, for it is too much trouble to have the proofs always present before us. We must acquire an easier belief, which is that of habit. With no violence, art or argument it makes us believe things, and so inclines all our faculties to this belief that our soul naturally falls into it. When we believe only by the strength of our conviction and the automaton is inclined to believe the opposite, that is not enough. We must therefore make both parts of us believe: the mind by reasons, which need to be seen only once in a lifetime, and the automaton by habit, and not allowing it any inclination to the contrary: *Incline my heart.* (821)

The life of faith can involve great struggle — struggle against the habits that would keep us from belief or from serving God, habits that are naturally ours as creatures in this world. It is made possible only by the forming of new habits to displace the old. It is these new habits, this new form of life, that Pascal urges on us as the only way ultimately of achieving complete and properly meaningful lives. Christian faith, he believes, is a path to God and, in the light of God's truth, a way of making sense of it all. It is a way of the heart.

In a series of notes presenting evidences for Christianity, Pascal has a list of topics that ends in an interesting way:

> PROOFS. — 1. The Christian religion, by the fact of being established, by establishing itself so firmly and so gently, though so contrary to nature — 2. The holiness, sublimity and humility of a Christian soul — 3. The miracles of holy Scripture — 4. Jesus Christ in particular — 5. The apostles in particular — 6. Moses and the prophets in particular — 7. The Jewish people — 8. Prophecies — 9. Perpetuity: no religion enjoys perpetuity — 10. Doctrine, accounting for everything — 11. The holiness of this law — 12. By the order of the world.
>
> Without any doubt after this, considering the nature of life and of this religion, we ought not to resist the inclination to follow it if our hearts are so inclined: and it is certain that there are no grounds for laughing at those who do follow it. (482)

There is no indication here that Pascal sees the evidence as able to coerce belief or to plant faith in everyone who considers it. The assessment of the role of evidence is much more modest than that. What is paramount is the inclination of the heart.

II

LOVE, LIFE, AND GOD

WHAT in this life is more elusive than happiness? Maybe nothing. Everyone wants it, but few seem to attain it. Perhaps there are some things *as* elusive as happiness. Wisdom, for one. Peace, for another. Some would suggest that these three items belong on an endangered species list for possible states of human existence. And it could very well be that their similar degree of elusiveness is no coincidence. Wisdom may be a prerequisite for happiness, at least for happiness of any stable or enduring sort. And both may be necessary conditions for peace, at least for any stable or enduring peace. A person who is not wise cannot be truly happy. And a person who is not truly happy cannot be at peace, either with himself or with others around him.

A life devoid of wisdom, happiness, and peace is a life unfulfilled. And a life unfulfilled long enough is a life of desperation. Pascal believed that there is enough wisdom available to us to shed light on this most desperate condition and to save us from it, if we will just take that measure of wisdom to heart. He seemed to think that the key to human happiness and a fulfilling peace is to be found hidden within what we can call "the economy of love." What do we love? How do we give our love? What do we love above all else? Becoming clear on the answers to these questions is crucial if we want to understand our lives. Giving the right answers is crucial if we want to live a good life — a life of wisdom, happiness, and peace.

To ask about love is not just to ask about an emotion or a feeling. And it's not just to ask about an attitude. To ask about what and how we love is to ask about how we perceive reality with our hearts and about how we commit our lives, how we order our hopes, and how we direct our energies. Within the bounds of human existence and beyond, the topic of love is one of unsurpassed importance. What and how we love will determine whether in this life we wander about hopelessly lost in the woods or whether, on the contrary, we move ahead in the direction of ultimate human fulfillment, gathering a harvest of wisdom, happiness, and peace as we go.

On the topic of love, Pascal had a good deal to say. And most of what he said is filled with deep insight. But he spoke as a wounded healer. Pascal was a person who had experienced problems with love. The least admirable episodes in his life, occurring prior to the time during which he wrote the *Pensées,* seem to have arisen out of the petulant imperiousness of an overweening self-love and, on one occasion, out of the grasping acquisitiveness of an inordinate love of money. Pascal was a very smart man, and he realized this. In argument with intellectual adversaries, he could be quite arrogant. He was not one to suffer fools gladly. And he came to expect the tremendous recognition he had received. He once argued with his sister over an inheritance and her desire to give her own share to the church. He learned about the value of humility and consideration of others the hard way, by experiencing the ultimately unsatisfying consequences of a contrary form of life. Because of this — because of his own errors and failings, from which

he eventually recoiled in disgust — he sometimes makes remarks about self-love and the love of material things that sound
very extreme, even offensive to modern ears. He can be so
negative. I believe he does sometimes go too far in his attempt
to articulate needed correctives to the unfortunate patterns of
thought and love that so easily entrap us. But he always leads
us into the neighborhood of some legitimate and important
insight we can embrace.

Consider, for example, the following somewhat enigmatic
remark:

Sinners lick the dust, that is, love earthly pleasures. (801)

This is certainly a vivid and memorable remark. What an image!
I see my English Springer Spaniel, just having finished a rare
treat of leftovers from the dinner table licking his bowl way
beyond spotless, licking the floor around his bowl. Not enough!
Not enough! More! More!

It's clear to any reader that Pascal means to be making a
disparaging remark concerning the love of earthly pleasures.
But what, exactly, is he saying, and why does he say it? Consider
the phrase "Sinners lick the dust." Does Pascal mean to say
that all sinners lick the dust? Does he mean to imply that all
dust lickers are sinners? And is that because he thinks that dust
licking itself is sinful? What exactly is this metaphor meant to
convey? It's hard to use the phrase so many times without
getting a bit of a dry tongue.

I think Pascal's legitimate point is this: we are cut off from
God, and so we are cut off from the source of all true satisfaction. We were created to live in a proper relationship to God,
and bereft of that proper relation we have need. Moreover, our
need is infinite. The place in our hearts created for an infinite
God cannot be filled with any finite creature. Without a proper

relation to the Creator of this world, nothing in the world can truly satisfy us. Everything we grasp crumbles to dust. And what do we do? Do we turn away? No, we lick the dust. In our blind desperation, we lick the dust. And does this satisfy? Of course not. We are pathetic in our inability, or unwillingness, to learn from experience that nothing in this world alone can satisfy.

But many things give us pleasure. And, says Pascal, we love earthly pleasures. He is dismissive about this, equating it with licking the dust. Why? The image is of someone desperate for satisfaction or, if not for that, at least for squeezing every drop of pleasure out of life. Everyone enjoys pleasure. That is true by definition. Everyone likes it. There can't be anything wrong with what is true by definition. But to like or enjoy something is not quite the same thing as to love it. We use the word *love* so casually. Perhaps far too casually. To love something is to prize it highly and to commit oneself to its preservation or cultivation. To love something is to orient your life, at least in part, around it. The paradigm of love is, of course, a relationship of absolute commitment between people. But can't it hold between people and things? In one passage, Pascal says,

> Christians know the true God and do not love earthly things. (289)

Is this true? Do Christians really not love earthly things? Well, we certainly *say* we do, quite often. "I love my fountain pens." "I love these shoes." "I love the sun." But of course this is all hyperbole. It is Pascal's view that we should not literally love anything that is merely of this world. An argument in favor of this view can be constructed that we can call *The Disproportionality Argument:*

(1) Whatever you truly love is something you orient your life around.

(2) You should not orient your life around something inadequate.

(3) Your life is eternal, but all things merely of this world are temporary.

(4) The temporary is not an adequate basis for the eternal.

So,

(5) You should not orient your life around anything that is merely of this world.

and thus

(6) You should not truly love anything that is merely of this world.

Remember, we are using the word *love* to represent the highest sort of commitment, an orientation that is, in Pascal's sense, a matter of the heart. In laying out the argument I have used the phrase "truly love" to keep us mindful of this.

There are denizens of this world that, from a Christian point of view, are not "merely of this world." People, for example. And there are activities, endeavors, and employments to be engaged in here that are not "merely of this earth." Caring, for example. And play. Perhaps even philosophy.

I remember vividly a student who once came back to visit me a year or two after his graduation from Notre Dame. He had been working in government and was very concerned about issues of war and peace. Over lunch, he talked about a well-known physician who had given up her medical practice in

Boston to work to rid the world of nuclear weapons. He reminded me of her conviction that all her work of sewing up
cuts, bandaging fractures, setting broken bones, clearing up
sore throats, all her work of healing would be completely un-
done by a nuclear holocaust, the sort of catastrophe the world
would continue moving closer and closer to with the continued
buildup of nuclear arsenals. So she decided that the ultimate
health care concern now required that she devote herself to
speaking and writing about nuclear issues. The young man then
complimented me on my speaking and writing abilities and
asked very pointedly why I had not done the same thing. Why
did I continue to teach and write on issues of skepticism, God,
free will, the soul, life after death, and the nature of religious
belief? I could devote myself instead full-time to the effort to
rid the world of nuclear weapons.

I explained that, for all my strong desire that the world not
continue to tremble in the shadow of such a terrible threat, I
was not convinced that even the worst nuclear catastrophe
would undo the work I am trying to do as a philosopher. I
believe that I am discovering, and am helping others to discover,
eternal truths, however feeble our grasp of them might be. And
in doing what I am trying to do for myself and others, I believe
I am ministering to the soul, which is of eternal value and will
have an eternal existence. If I am right, then not even the heat
death of the entire physical universe will completely undo the
little work I can do as a philosopher. Plato told us, and he had
it on the best authority from Socrates, that philosophy is a
preparation for death. This sounds morbid, but it's not. From
Plato's point of view, philosophy is not preparing us for an end
so much as for a great beginning. There are endeavors in this
world that are not merely of this world.

But anything that is merely of this world is not something
we should build our lives on. It is a foundation of sand. And

too many of us do this. Every occupation is noble insofar as it contributes to the welfare of people. Every relationship to an object in this world is appropriate if it contributes to some measure of true human flourishing. But if some endeavor or relationship involves building the edifice of your life on an inadequate, unstable, temporary foundation, it is wrong and should be avoided. Truly loving anything that is merely of this world is, according to Pascal, wrong. Persons are eternal. So the building of right relationships among people is always appropriate. It has even been said that the whole of morality can be summed up in a simple piece of advice: "Love people, use things; don't love things or use people." Whether that does capture the whole of morality or not, it clearly captures something of fundamental importance from a Pascalian, or Christian, point of view. The strongest sort of commitment should be directed only to a person, never to a thing.

Recall Pascal's words precisely for a moment:

Sinners lick the dust, that is, love earthly pleasures.

It may be significant that he disparages the love of earthly *pleasures* in particular. Many people love not so much the things of this world themselves but the pleasures they can bring us. And this is even worse.

From a well-balanced Christian point of view, there is absolutely nothing wrong with enjoying the things of this world and enjoying them immensely. There is absolutely nothing wrong with the experience of pleasure. It is good. It is even a good worth pursuing. But it is not a good worth pursuing at all costs. It is not an overriding good. It is not an appropriate focal point for a human life. It is more like a wonderful by-product of human activity, which ought to have other goals. To engage in the orientation of the soul and complete commitment of the heart that would, from Pascal's perspective, count as *loving* earthly pleasures would be a perversion symptomatic of human wretchedness.

Loving things that are merely of this world at least can involve appreciating them as they are in themselves, for all its untoward extremity. And it is good to appreciate the goods of this world. But to love earthly pleasures is to orient your life not around an appreciation of the things in the world themselves for what they are in themselves but is rather to orient your life around what they can do for you. In the eyes of a lover of pleasure, all the world is an instrument, a tool of the self. The value of anything consists in what it can bring the self. Love of pleasure is inappropriate precisely because it is a function of an inappropriate love of self. And there is nothing Pascal thunders against more loudly than a wrongful love of self.

There is nothing in Pascal's notes so shocking to first-time readers as his strident denunciations of self-love and a completely unexpected recommendation of self-hate. He says in one place that

We must love God alone and hate ourselves alone. (373)

What a sentiment! Many of the social and psychological problems in the world today can be traced to people's lacking a proper self-esteem. There are books, articles, workshops, and videotapes promoting self-esteem. "I'm O.K., You're O.K." we're supposed to say, and we're not free to acknowledge the latter until we see the former. And doesn't even Jesus himself in the New Testament command "Love your neighbor *as yourself*"? I can't love my neighbor *unless* I love myself according to this command. So what in the world could Pascal possibly have in mind in saying that we must *hate* ourselves alone?

To come to an understanding of what Pascal could have meant that is plausible, and even insightful, we have to do a little detective work throughout the *Pensées*. We can come up with an interpretation of this statement that makes a lot of sense and that is a much-needed corrective to a tendency we all have deep down. Whether it is all Pascal intended, we cannot be sure. But, again, as in our reflections on every other vital issue Pascal brings to our attention, our aim is not so much to nail down for certain exactly what he meant to convey in his remarks as it is to ask whether he may again have led us into the neighborhood of some initially surprising but deeply important truth. To see where he is leading us, however, we need to look for some clues.

First, let's consider a rather lengthy excerpt from a longer passage on self-love:

The nature of self-love and of this human self is to love only self and consider only self. But what is it to do? It cannot prevent the object of its love from being full of faults and wretchedness: it wants to be great and sees that it is small; it wants to be happy and sees that it is wretched; it wants to be perfect and sees that it is full of imperfections; it wants to be the object of men's love and esteem and sees that its faults deserve only their dislike and contempt. The predicament in which it thus finds itself arouses in it the most unjust and criminal passion that could possibly be imagined, for it conceives a deadly hatred for the truth which rebukes it and convinces it of its faults. It would like to do away with this truth, and not being able to destroy it as such, it destroys it, as best it can, in the consciousness of itself and others; that is, it takes care to hide its faults both from itself and others, and cannot bear to have them pointed out or noticed.

It is no doubt an evil to be full of faults, but it is a still greater evil to be full of them and unwilling to recognize them, since this entails the further evil of deliberate self-delusion. We do not want others to deceive us; we do not think it right for them to want us to esteem them more than they deserve; it is therefore not right either that we should deceive them and want them to esteem us more than we deserve. (978)

Self-love comes naturally to us. We center our world around the self, its needs, its wants, and its values. The care and cultivation of the self becomes our consuming passion. And yet, cut off from God our Creator, we have faults, serious flaws, and weaknesses. Focusing only on ourselves, we find ourselves unlovable. But we need to be loved and take it upon ourselves first and foremost to meet that need. So we suppress the truth about our faults and flaws. And even worse yet, we also connive to convince others that we are without these faults and flaws and therefore are lovable. We deceive others as we deceive ourselves, because that is necessary for successful self-deception. We find it easiest to believe what others believe. So, if we want to believe a lie, we must convince others that it is true. We need comrades in delusion.

Now the fact is that we are lovable despite our faults. But one of our faults is our failure to see that. From a Christian point of view, we are lovable as the creations of a good God, made in God's image. If we do not enjoy that point of view, we naturally fall into that pattern of thought and behavior Pascal identifies. In our desperation to think of all of life as centered around our selves, we insist that others center their lives around us.

It is untrue that we are worthy to be loved by others. It is unfair that we should want such a thing. If we were born reasonable and impartial, with a knowledge of ourselves and others, we should not give our wills this bias. However, we are born with it, and so we are born unfair.

For everything tends towards itself: this is contrary to all order.

The tendency should be towards the general, and the bias towards self is the beginning of all disorder, in war, politics, economics, in man's individual body.

The will is therefore depraved. If the members of natural and civil communities tend to the good of the whole body, the communities themselves should tend towards another more general body of which they are members. We should therefore tend towards the general. (421)

He adds in another place that

Each man is everything to himself, for with his death everything is dead for him. That is why each of us thinks he is everything to everyone. We must not judge nature by ourselves, but by its own standards. (668)

The inclination to self-love is natural to us in our condition, and it is a vortex, pulling everything in toward itself. The bias toward self that is self-aggrandizement will inevitably rip any fabric of human relations asunder. When each self wants to center the world in itself, the world of all selves is inevitably torn to bits. In such a world the abandonment of wisdom has made peace and happiness impossible.

In one place, Pascal represents a dialogue between himself and one of his friends who was a well-known worldly gambler and a man of apparently suave sophistication. The dialogue begins with Pascal saying that

'The self is hateful. You cover it up, Mitton, but that does not mean that you take it away. So you are still hateful.'

'Not so, because by being obliging to everyone as we are, we give them no more cause to hate us.'

'True enough if the only hateful thing about the self were the unpleasantness it caused us.

'But if I hate it because it is unjust that it should make itself the centre of everything, I shall go on hating it.

'In a word the self has two characteristics. It is unjust in itself for making itself the center of everything: it is a nuisance to others in that it tries to subjugate them, for each self is the enemy of all others and would like to tyrannize them. You take away the nuisance, but not the injustice.

'And thus, you do not make it pleasing to those who hate it for being unjust; you only make it pleasing to unjust people who no longer see it as their enemy. Thus you remain unjust, and can only please unjust people.' (597)

Strong words indeed. Further amplifying the same theme, he says elsewhere that

Anyone who does not hate the self-love within him and the instinct which leads him to make himself into a God must be really blind. Who can fail to see that there is nothing so contrary to justice and truth? For it is false that we deserve this position and unjust and impossible to attain it, because everybody demands the same thing. We are thus born into an obviously unjust situation from which we cannot escape but from which we must escape.

However, no [other] religion has observed that this is a sin, that it is innate in us, or that we are obliged to resist it, let alone thought of providing a cure. (617)

What is the cure Pascal speaks of here? He indicates what it is like this:

The Christians' God is a God who makes the soul aware that

he is its sole good: that in him alone can it find peace; that
only in loving him can it find joy: and who at the same time
fills it with loathing for the obstacles which hold it back and
prevent it from loving God with all its might. Self-love and
concupiscence, which hold it back, are intolerable. This God
makes the soul aware of this underlying self-love which is
destroying it, and which he alone can cure. (460)

Finally, and most startlingly, we find Pascal saying:

The true and only virtue is therefore to hate ourselves, for
our concupiscence makes us hateful, and to seek for a being
really worthy of love in order to love him. But as we cannot
love what is outside us, we must love a being who is within
us but is not our own self. And this is true for every single
person. Now only the universal being is of this kind: the
kingdom of God is within us, and is both ourselves and not
ourselves. (564)

We now have almost all we need to understand Pascal on
self-love and self-hate. We have almost all we need to understand Pascal on love, life, and God.

Let us get the passage from which we began again before us:

We must love God alone and hate ourselves alone. (373)

I believe that the insight to be found here is revealed by a matter
of emphasis in how this sentence is to be read. What are we
to hate, according to Pascal? Ourselves? *"Ourselves alone."* We
are to hate the self-centeredness of the self cut off from God.
We are to hate the insular autonomy of the self as it sets itself
up against every other self as well as against God, attempting
to usurp the position that is properly God's alone. God alone
is different from any other self alone. God's being is somehow
inclusive. Pascal refers to God as "the universal being" (564).

It is impossible genuinely to love God without appropriately relating to God's creation, other selves and one's own self included. And this is not just the ultimate instance of "Love me, love my dog." For the image of God is within every person. Everything exists only through God's will. God is not just a remote creator, transcending and existing outside his creation. He is immanent throughout the world as well, omnipresent in being as well as in power and knowledge. To love God is to love unity in its ultimate instance. To love the self alone is to create and embrace divisiveness, a divisiveness that is unjust and destructive and wrong.

In other passages, Pascal speaks of a healthy and proper self-love that is not divisive and of a love for other human beings that is both appropriate and fulfilling. He says, for example, that "Christianity makes men both happy and lovable" (426), and he says from the heart "I love all men" (931). He even speaks of "the love we owe ourselves":

> *Members. Begin there.* In order to control the love we owe ourselves, we must imagine a body full of thinking members (for we are members of the whole), and see how each member ought to love itself, etc. (368)

Elsewhere he says, simply,

> Imagine a body of thinking members. (371)

And in the very next note, he elaborates:

> To be a member is to have no life, no being and no movement except through the spirit of the body and for the body. The separated member, no longer seeing the body to which it belongs, has only a wasting and moribund being left. However, it believes itself to be a whole, and, seeing no body on

which it depends, believes itself to be dependent only on itself and tries to make itself its own centre and body. But, not having in itself any principle of life, it only wanders about and becomes bewildered at the uncertainty of its existence, quite conscious that it is not the body and yet not seeing that it is [a] member of a body. Eventually, when it comes to know itself, it has returned home, as it were, and only loves itself for the body's sake. It deplores its past aberrations.

It could not by its very nature love anything else except for selfish reasons and in order to enslave it, because each thing loves itself more than anything else.

But in loving the body it loves itself, because it has no being except in the body, through the body, and for the body. *But he that is joined unto the Lord is one spirit* [I Cor. VI.17]. (372)

Pascal goes on to say that "we love ourselves because we are members of Christ." There is a proper self-love, a love that does not isolate or exclude. It is a love of self in solidarity with others who are themselves ultimately fellow members of the body of the universal being, in solidarity with all. This is a beautiful New Testament picture that Pascal takes up and uses in a powerful way. His basic point is that love should never be divisive or exclusivist; it should always be unifying and inclusive. This is a point worth repeating: love should never be divisive or exclusivist; it should always be unifying and inclusive. We are essentially social beings. We cannot have a proper self-identity apart from proper relations to others. We cannot have a proper self-love without a proper love of others. And in the last analysis, the kind of self-love Pascal hates is at best a quite degenerate form of love. For what Pascal hates is the egoistic exclusivist commitment to self that raises the self up over and against all others. And this is both destructive and, finally, self-destructive as well. That's the great irony. But genuine love for a self always wills the best for that self. So an inappropriate fixation with your own self, in which you seek to love yourself at the expense of or to the neglect of others, is no true love at all. It is sometimes said that love is blind. But real love cannot be blind. In order for anyone to engage in that affair of the heart that is genuine love, some measure of wisdom is needed. And it is only a significant measure of wisdom that can allow for and control a proper, firm, and committed self-love.

The meaning of Pascal's statement that "We must love God alone and hate ourselves alone" must surely be judged in context. And the most immediate context is provided by the previous note (372), in which he delineates the form of proper self-love. What we must hate is the self standing alone. What we must love is God, and God in all, and all in God. This is Pascal's prescription for salvation from the madness of the world. And that is because it is the Christian prescription for salvation from the madness of the world, in self-imposed exile from God. To love God, and to love God as God reaches out to love us in Christ, is the key. This is the beginning of wisdom, which is the condition of peace, which alone can provide for the happiness of all human beings.

What Pascal is recommending to us is a reorientation of our lives, a wager of the heart, a repositioning of our minds. What do we love? What do we desire? What do we hope? What do we think? In one place he writes,

> Man is obviously made for thinking. Therein lies all his dignity and his merit; and his whole duty is to think as he ought. Now the order of thought is to begin with ourselves, and with our author and our end.
>
> Now what does the world think about? Never about that, but about dancing, playing the lute, singing, writing verse, tilting at the ring, etc., and fighting, becoming king, without thinking what it means to be a king or to be a man. (620)

Most of us are, to some degree or another, trapped in habits of thought and desire that block us from seeing the truth, that prevent us from perceiving God with our hearts, and thus that keep us from finding our way in this life. Pascal wants to help free us from these inhibiting and destructive habits. He wants to open us up to genuine fulfillment. He wants to lead us into true understanding. He wants to bring us to God.

And Pascal believes that once we are launched into a Christian life, fundamental things should change. He says, for example,

> Let us change the rule we have hitherto adopted for judging what is good. We took our own will as rule; let us now take the will of God. (948)

From this new point of view, the world — God's world — is charged with significance. In accordance with this new way of thinking, Pascal would advise us to

> Do small things as if they were great, because of the majesty of Christ, who does them in us and lives our life, and great things as if they were small and easy, because of his almighty power. (919)

And, surely, acting in this way would endow us all with greatness. Focusing on God, perceiving God with the heart, orienting all our values, attitudes, emotions, desires, hopes, and dreams finally around God and God's will for us, we become great. And that is of great benefit, as displayed by this image:

> Great and small are liable to the same accidents, the same annoyance, the same passion, but one is at the top of the wheel and the other near its centre, and thus less shaken by the same movements. (705)

With wisdom comes inner peace, and with peace, true happiness.

Pascal is convinced that the wisdom we need is to be found first and foremost in Jesus the Christ, the Wisdom of God:

> Not only do we only know God through Jesus Christ, but we only know ourselves through Jesus Christ; we only know life and death through Jesus Christ. Apart from Jesus Christ we cannot know the meaning of our life or our death, of God or of ourselves.
>
> Thus without Scripture, whose only object is Christ, we know nothing, and can see nothing but obscurity and confusion in the nature of God and in nature itself. (417)

Pascal does not endorse a vaguely, generically religious vision. His is a clearly focused Christian vision of the world, powerfully sketched and powerfully recommended. He was hoping that he could write something to help us to see the truth and importance of this vision. He wanted to help us make sense of it all. He wanted to help us to begin to move in the right direction to be able, eventually, to join the great company of the saints of God. But Pascal knew he could not do it for us alone. And we cannot succeed alone. He says, quite profoundly, that

> To make a man a saint, grace is certainly needed, and anyone who doubts this does not know what a saint, or a man, really is. (869)

It is only by the grace of God that faith, reason, and the meaning of life can finally come together in mutual fulfillment.

This is a powerful vision for human existence, and it is one well worth our greatest attention.

INDEX

213